TURTLES&
TORTOISES
OF THE
WORLD

TURTLES & TORTOISES OF THE WORLD

David Alderton

Photographs by
Tony Tilford

BLANDFORD

Blandford Press
London   New York   Sydney

Turtles & Tortoises of the World

Paperback edition first published in the UK 1993
by Blandford, a Cassell imprint

Cassell plc
Wellington House
125 Strand
London WC2R 0BB

Reprinted 1997 & 1998
Previously published in hardback by Blandford in 1988
Reprinted 1992

Distributed in the United States by Sterling Publishing Co., Inc.,
387 Park Avenue South, New York, NY 10016–8810

**A Cataloguing-in-Publication Data entry for this title
is available from the British Library**

ISBN 0-7137-2391-2

Typeset by Graficraft Typesetters Ltd, Hong Kong
Printed in Hong Kong by Colorcraft Ltd

Contents

Acknowledgements

All photographs were taken by Tony Tilford (Press-tige Pictures, Cringleford, Norwich, Norfolk), except Plate 11 by Tony Silva, and Plates 20, 26, 42, 44, 45, 46, 47, 48, 50 and 89 by the author. Line illustrations by Michael Alderton.

Grateful thanks are extended to the many people who have assisted in the preparation of this book, especially the following for their invaluable help: Dr Chris Andrews and Dave Ball (London Zoo); Ken Doulton; John Ebbage; Rita Hemsley; Dick Hull; Dick Klees; Dr David Madge; Pat Murray (British Chelonia Group); Kathryn Packer; Bryan Peck; Phil Reid; Rotterdam Zoo; Raymond Sawyer; Tony Silva; Robin Smith (Tas Valley Koi, Norfolk); Simon Tilford; Zuza Vrbova.

For Zuza
with special thanks

Preface

People react differently to different creatures, especially in the case of reptiles. While snakes often provoke a strong sense of dislike from the casual observer, tortoises and turtles attract a much more positive response. This is obvious from walking around any large store. Here, a variety of household objects and toys portraying tortoises will almost certainly be seen. It is perhaps surprising, therefore, that so few books have been written about this group of reptiles, especially as some species have been so widely kept as pets for many years.

The history of human interaction with chelonians is, sadly, littered with numerous instances of careless, greedy exploitation, as exemplified by the giant tortoises, whole populations of which were destroyed by sailors visiting the Galapagos and Aldabran Islands during past centuries. Fresh-water species have also suffered, as shown by the case of diamondback terrapin, which was brought to the verge of extinction in order to satisfy the appetites of American gourmets.

Today, however, the greatest concern is focused on the seven marine species of turtle, of which five are presently threatened with extinction. The lifestyle of these chelonians renders them uniquely susceptible to human interference. I shall always remember my first sight of a sea turtle swimming in the wild, over the Barrier Reef, off the coast of Queensland, Australia. The agility and elegance of this creature underwater is in total contrast to the slow, cumbersome individual which drags herself onto land to lay her eggs. Here, in what is virtually another world, they are almost totally defenceless, and particularly vulnerable to the effects of human predation.

But it is simply not enough to try to conserve turtles by attempting to prevent their capture. The hunting of turtles has been ingrained in many cultures for centuries. If turtles are to be conserved for future generations, it is their economic value that offers their salvation. The transfer of eggs for artificial incubation has been used in the past, with hatchlings then being released into the sea, but this is now accepted as a highly inefficient method of attempting to increase the numbers of reproductively active turtles in the wild. Out of the thousands released, only a minute percentage will survive the hazardous years to maturity, returning to breed, perhaps decades later.

Commercial ranching now appears to offer potentially the most effective means of increasing the numbers of these reptiles which have graced the world's oceans for nearly 200 million years. A considerable amount of knowledge has been gained about the captive-rearing of turtles under these conditions. Now it is possible to rear hatchlings to maturity in a comparatively short space of time. The successful release of these turtles back to the oceans would offer a more rapid and effective means of repopulation than releasing vast numbers of hatchlings. The demand for turtle products, essentially one of the major factors in the decline of these reptiles, could also be met from captive-reared animals, rather than by the continual capture of wild individuals. Whether westernised sensibilities will allow this to happen remains to the seen.

It is significant that while such ranching schemes for crocodilians are widely accepted, the concept of rearing any turtles for slaughter remains highly controversial, even if this system of management represents the logical step forward in ensuring the conservation of the species itself. The turtle issue reveals the misplaced emotional fervour which presently threatens to undermine the overall credibility of the conservation movement. It would, indeed, be a tragic irony if a combination of misplaced human sympathy and continued hunting were to prove the two major forces which led to the extinction of any species of turtle.

David Alderton
Brighton, East Sussex, 1988

Chapter 1
Chelonians and Humans

The description 'chelonian' is derived from the classificatory name 'Chelonia.' While the group of reptiles variously known as tortoises, turtles and terrapins are instantly recognisable because of their distinctive shells, the actual terms used to describe these creatures which form the order Chelonia are far from clear. In Britain, the description of 'tortoise' tends to be applied to those species which are primarily terrestrial in their habits. Turtles, in contrast, are predominantly aquatic, and certain members of this group are also called terrapins. It appears that this description, which originated with the native Indians of North America, was then adopted by the early European settlers. They applied it to chelonians which were caught for food, especially species found in brackish waters, such as the diamondback terrapin (*Malaclemys terrapin*).

Plate 1   The diamondback terrapin (*Malaclemys terrapin*) was brought to the verge of extinction in the early years of this century because of its popularity as a gourmet's dish, costing as much as $120 per dozen. They have since recovered in numbers to a large extent.

Plate 2 Confusion surrounds the common terms used to describe chelonians. In Britain, terrestrial and semi-terrestrial forms are usually known as tortoises, whereas in North America and Australia, all species tend to be termed turtles. This problem over nomenclature is crystallised in the case of the North American box turtles (*Terrapene* spp) which are more commonly encountered on land, and thus often known in Britain as tortoises.

Throughout North America and most of the remainder of the English-speaking world, however, it is the term 'turtle' which is often used as an all-embracing description of these unique reptiles. This word is undoubtedly a more recent addition to the language, as it is clear that up to the sixteenth century, the description 'tortoise' was also applied to aquatic species.

British sailors venturing into the Caribbean waters, following Spanish and Portuguese explorers, soon adopted their descriptions for the marine chelonian species which they encountered. It seems more than likely that the Spanish word *tortuga* was the origin of the term 'turtle'. Writing about his expedition to South America in 1595, Sir Walter Raleigh refers to the *tortuges* and how both these creatures and their eggs were eaten by the crew. At that stage, marine turtles were far more numerous than they are today, and it has been suggested that their population could have exceeded 50 million turtles, compared with the estimated number of 10,000 in the area today.

Turtles and art

Chelonians have tended to hold a special place in human affections, in spite of being heavily persecuted down the ages. Most ancient cultures feature representations of turtles and tortoises in their art, in some cases also utilising tortoiseshell for various purposes. This material is actually obtained from the hawksbill turtle (*Eretmochelys imbricata*), being the scutes, or outer layer of the shell. Only the top part of the shell shows the richness of markings for which tortoiseshell has always been prized. In the living animal, however, the shell appears drab in comparison, often being discoloured by the attachment of marine creatures such as barnacles.

Hawksbill turtles, presumably captured in the Red Sea, were highly valued by the ancient Egyptians. Their shell was particularly popular for the manufacture of bracelets and knife handles. The appearance of these turtles is not portrayed in Egyptian art, however, although the African soft-shell (*Trionyx triunguis*) is featured on tombs. Gradually, it appears that these turtles acquired a malevolent image. This seems to have persisted, at least in part, through the days of the Greek empire, when the word describing tortoises meant 'dweller in Hell'. Early Christians

Plate 3   Illegal trade in turtle products still takes place, in spite of international attempts to control it. This is part of the haul confiscated by customs officers from travellers passing through Rotterdam.

frequently portrayed chelonians in battle with cockerels, symbolising a battle between the force of evil and the need for vigilance. It appears that the slow gait of the tortoise contributed to its unpopularity at this time. St Jerome refers to the tortoise, with its ponderous movements, as being burdened under the weight of sin.

In China, the tortoise was also significant in religious circles. The markings on the top of its shell were believed to reveal the future for those who could read the signs. The image of the tortoise was incorporated into a solid form as a pedestal during the Sung dynasty, probably as early as AD 990, because of its wisdom.

Practical representations of chelonians actually date back several millennia in China. Here, the Emperor Hwang-ti had the emblem of a snake entwined with a tortoise, some 2,500 years BC. These creatures were said to protect one against evil forces, and to keep danger away, so that flags showing this emblem were carried both in front of and behind the emperor's entourage. It was believed, at this stage, that all chelonians were exclusively female, and that the snake was necessary for breeding purposes. The image of the tortoise and serpent, although it has largely disappeared from Chinese culture today, is also featured in Indian legends.

Plate 4   A variety of tortoise artifacts. Tortoises have been represented in the art of most cultures which have come into contact with them. The distinctive appearance and long lifespan of these reptiles have also formed the basis of numerous folklore stories in many parts of the world.

The term 'tortoise' also became an insult of the worst kind when used to describe another person. This seems to have arisen because the *lo hu*, who were considered outcasts from society during the Tang dynasty, were forced to wrap their heads in green cloth, which then resembled the appearance of a tortoise.

Longevity

In neighbouring Japan, chelonians were regarded as symbols of happiness and good fortune, because of their potentially long lifespan. Representations of tortoises were common gifts, particularly at weddings, to wish a long and happy life to the couple. Chinese attitudes towards tortoises were also apparent in Japan. These chelonians were viewed as being responsible for protecting all other creatures with shells. Various references in eastern mythology describe how the earth was supported by tortoises. In China, Joka, the sister of Fukki, a mythological Chinese figure, was said to have taken the tortoise's legs for this purpose, when a giant destroyed one of the pillars of Heaven, which kept the world in place. Indian legend viewed the tortoise as supporting an elephant, which in turn supported the world on its back. The Japanese portrayed a tortoise as carrying the sacred mountain of Horai on its back. Since Horai was inhabited by immortals, this appears to be a clear reference to the chelonian's potentially long lifespan.

This characteristic feature of chelonians has fascinated human imagination right down to the present day. While precise figures are rather difficult to establish, it seems clear that the lifespan of these reptiles typically exceeds that of other vertebrates. The record for longevity is said to belong to a radiated tortoise (*Geochelone radiata*) which was a gift from Captain Cook to the King of Tonga. After an eventful life, during which it was in collision with a cart and exposed to a couple of forest fires, this tortoise was said to have been over 189 years old when it finally died in 1966. As there is no record of this gift in Captain Cook's writings, however, it is impossible to authenticate this story.

Better documented is the case of Marion's tortoises. The French explorer, Marion de Fresne, visited the Seychelles in 1776, and obtained five native tortoises during this period. These were of the now extinct giant species known as *Geochelone sumeirei*. They were transferred to the nearby island of Mauritius, and remained there when the British took this territory from the French in 1810. The tortoises became a popular feature, living at the Royal Artillery barracks. The last survivor finally died in 1918, when it became trapped in a gun emplacement. This meant that it must have been at least 152 years old, and was probably nearer 200, assuming it was an adult on its arrival in Mauritius.

Size is no indication of the potential lifespan of chelonians, as small species can also live for a long time. The box turtles of the genus *Terrapene* appear to have a long natural lifespan. It seems that it used to be a popular pastime to carve initials and a date on the shells of these turtles in various parts of North America, notably in the north-east of the United States. Although a system of this kind is clearly open to abuse, there do appear to be some genuine records of centenarian box turtles as a result. A high proportion of these have been found in New England, Rhode Island and Connecticut.

One particularly interesting and apparently valid case of extreme longevity involved a box turtle popularly known as 'Hope Valley Turtle, Old 1844', which may have lived for as long as 138 years. He was discovered on a farm by a boy who noticed there were two different dates and initials etched into the plastron. Subsequent investigation revealed that amongst those working on this farm back in 1844 had been a young man called Edward Barber Kenyon, who was then 19 years old. This appears to explain the initials 'E.B.K.' and the date. It was not possible to trace the other initials 'G.V.B.' alongside the date of 22 July 1860. However, two families, the Barbers and the Bitgoods, had lived on the farm, and a member of one of them could have engraved the turtle's shell. Box turtles are known not to range far afield, and so it is tempting to suppose that 'Old 1844' had remained in this area throughout his life. Since they are fully grown at 20 years old, there would be no distortion of any shell carving after this stage. This means that this box turtle would already have been at least two decades old when it was originally caught by Edward Kenyon: 'Old 1844' therefore became the oldest known living animal recorded in the United States.

This eastern box turtle (*Terrapene carolina*) may have been slightly younger than another individual, found in 1954 on Rhode Island, which bore the date '1836', along with the initial 'G'. A later inscription was dated 1890, but in spite of an intensive search, it was not possible to locate any trace of James S. Evans, whose name was etched alongside this later date. Another box turtle, also carrying the date of '1836' with various initials, featured in a newspaper article after its discovery in 1951, but again its history was impossible to ascertain.

One of the most romantic conclusions to a search for the possible authenticity of the carving on the shell of a box turtle began with the marking 'JRWIMA, June 16 78'. The researchers decided these must have been two sets of initials, possibly of sweethearts. A search of the local records in Kingston, Rhode Island revealed that there were, indeed, once a Jeremiah Robinson Wells and an Ida May Adams, although they never actually married.

A later inscription, 'GHA', accompanied by the date '89', on the same turtle, was probably made by a railroad supervisor, called George Henry Abbott. Indeed, the turtle itself, when found again in 1967, was actually wandering alongside the same railway track where Abbott had worked.

Aquatic turtles would appear to have slightly shorter lives than their more terrestrial counterparts. The figures which have been suggested are quite variable, however, and may be influenced by individual populations. Nevertheless, their life expectancy is likely to be in excess of 30 years, and can be as much as 70, at least in captivity. It seems likely that marine turtles may potentially live for over half a century, although, again, reliable records are sparse.

Turtles in literature

Chelonians have also featured in various stories which reflect their slow, but intelligent nature. The origins of the well-known Aesop's fable 'The Tortoise and The Hare' appear to reside in African legend. Here, chelonians in their various forms feature in many folklore tales. The Akamba people describe how a race took place between a tortoise and a fish eagle, to win the hand of a Kamba girl. The creatures were told by her father that the first to return with sea salt, setting off for the coast and returning before darkness fell on the same day, could marry his daughter.

The tortoise appeared reluctant to accept this challenge, but the eagle was keen for the race to take place. Agreeing to the tortoise's request, it was decided to defer the challenge for ten months. During this time, the tortoise secretly set off for the coast. The journey took five months, and as he passed other tortoises, the original tortoise asked for their help when the race finally took place. They were to station themselves in conspicuous places along the route, where they would be clearly visible to the eagle. Finally, after reaching the coast, the tortoise returned to his home, carrying sea salt.

When the race began, the eagle was surprised to see how fast the tortoise appeared to be moving. At various points, he called out to his competitor, '*Ngu iko?*', and the tortoise beneath acknowledged his presence. When he reached the shore, the eagle was amazed to find that the tortoise had apparently got there first, and was already gathering salt. The bird quickly collected his supply, and flew off before the tortoise left, being certain that he would win the race.

All this time, the tortoise against whom he was supposed to be racing, had been at home. As the chelonian spotted his rival heading back, he gathered the salt that he had collected five months before, and took it the short distance to the girl's father, before the eagle arrived. The tortoise was declared the winner, and the eagle realised that he had been deceived. The father of the girl was concerned that, in his anger, the bird was likely to seek out the tortoise and kill him. It was at this point that the tortoise promised he would leave the land and live in the water in the future, where the eagle would be unable to reach him.

A similar theme can be seen in the stories told by other African tribes, such as the Hottentot, although in this case, the victims were ostriches, rather than an eagle. It is probably significant that there are links in other tales between tortoises and hares, indeed they are used interchangeably in some cases, and this may explain the link in Aesop's fable.

The impact of the tortoise on human culture is such that in virtually every area where chelonians occur, they have been incorporated into the folklore of the native people. They feature quite prominently in creationist tales. The Buriats, a central Asian people, relate how, at the beginning of the world, there was no land, only water. God then decided to turn the large turtle over onto its back, and thus created the land. Similarly, there is another story as to how Mandishire, having created the world, was transformed into a huge turtle, and supported the floating land on his large shell. The origins of such stories can be traced back to ancient India, where the creator of the world was said to be in the form of a turtle.

The chelonian is still revered today as a sacred creature in some parts of the Indian sub-continent. Indeed, one species appears to have survived only because of this association. The black softshell (*Trionyx nigricans*) lives in a semi-wild state in a pond which forms part of the sacred shrine of Sultan Bagu Bastan, close to the town of Chittagong in Bangladesh. These turtles have become so tame that they will apparently come to feed from the hand, emerging at night to bask on a nearby hillock, where they also lay their eggs. The actual age of the colony is obscure, but certainly it has been in existence for well over a century, being described as long ago as 1875.

Another species which may have been kept in close proximity to religious institutions is the Siamese temple turtle (*Siebenrockiella crassicollis*). The distribution of these turtles includes Thailand (formerly Siam) and extends over the Malay Peninsula to the offshore islands of Borneo, Java and Sumatra.

Plate 5   Some turtles have assumed religious significance, being kept in a state of semi-liberty around temples and other religious institutions, especially in Asia. This is the Siamese temple turtle (*Siebenrockiella crassicollis*).

Chapter 2
Form and Function

The unmistakable appearance of chelonians results from their characteristic shell, which encases the whole of the body apart from the limbs, head and tail. The shell itself is usually a fairly rigid structure, although in a few cases, such as the soft-shelled turtles of the family Trionychidae, this covering has become softer.

General anatomy of the shell

The shell is divided into two parts, the upper surface being known as the carapace, and the lower described as the plastron. These two components are linked together for structural support by so-called bridges, located between the front and hind limbs on each side of the body.

The strength and rigidity of the shell itself results from an inner bony casing of fused plates, which in turn are covered by horny shields made of keratin and usually called 'scutes', or sometimes 'laminae', although

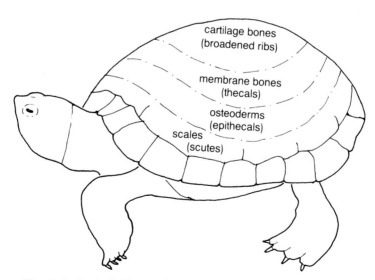

Fig. 1   The chelonian's shell comprises several layers, which increase its overall structural strength, although, in some cases, these layers may be reduced or absent. The scutes form the outer layer.

Plate 6   The characteristic shell of chelonians generally comprises two main layers. There is an inner, supporting bony casement which is covered with an outer layer of keratin. This contains the distinctive coloration and patterning of the species concerned.

this is a less applicable term. The actual pattern of these two layers varies, so that the joins in each section do not overlap. This serves to reinforce the overall protection provided by the shell. Indeed, in the centre of the carapace, there may be up to ten dermal plates covered by a single epidermal scute. Around the edge of the carapace, however, where the peripheral bones are relatively large, the situation may be reversed, with two scutes protecting a single bone. The carapace usually comprises about 50 bones, although individual variations do occur, both between species and, less commonly, between individuals. Modifications to the suprapygal bone, located at the rear end of the carapace, and the neurals, which run in parallel down both sides of the shell, are most common.

Plate 7   The distinctive rear hinges, and flared marginal shields, which can afford greater protection to the tortoise's hindquarters, are clearly seen here in this Home's hingeback (*Kinixys homeana*).

The structure of the plastron tends to be quite stable, in terms of both its bone and scute structure. Overall, the bony casing is surrounded by about 54 scutes, with 16 of these covering the plastron. The names of the scutes are derived essentially from anatomical landmarks, so that terms such as humeral, pectoral and anal give a clear indication of the position of the scute in question. The vertebral scutes on the carapace are those most likely to show variations, although, occasionally, the costals can also be affected.

Standard alterations to the shape of the marginal scutes are also not uncommon, as shown by the African genus *Kinixys*. Both Home's and the eroded hingeback tortoise (*K. homeana* and *K. erosa*) have flared marginals, especially around their rear quarters, in contrast to the smooth marginal profile of Bell's hingeback (*K. belliana*). In spite of such overall widespread uniformity in shell structure, however, chelonians showing deviations from the normal patterning associated with a particular species are not apparently handicapped in any way.

Growth of the scutes

The growth layer over the bony plates, from which the scutes develop, is formed from the epidermis, and is thus applied with nerve endings, like

Fig. 2 The typical arrangement of the scutes, seen here from both dorsal and ventral views. Note also the tympanum, which acts as the external ear.

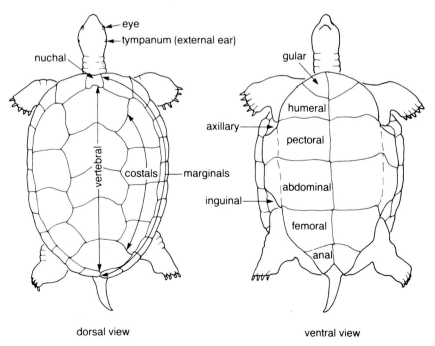

eye
tympanum (external ear)
nuchal
gular
humeral
axillary
pectoral
vertebral
costals
marginals
abdominal
inguinal
femoral
anal

dorsal view

ventral view

normal skin. It will also bleed if damaged. The Malpighian cells, responsible for the manufacture of keratin, here lie beneath the individual scutes. Growth occurs by the addition of further keratin to the base of the existing scute, leading to a gradual widening in its diameter.

A number of species, especially those found in temperate areas, such as the *Terrapene* box turtles, undergo set periods of growth during the warmer part of each year. A small ridge forms each time the expansion of the scute ceases, creating the pattern of growth rings, or annuli, which are visible on the shell. Counting these rings is a popular but unreliable means of ageing chelonians, especially in the case of young hatchlings. They are likely to show a number of growth rings before even one year of age, which do not, therefore, represent annual growth.

As the chelonian becomes older, it would seem likely that the centre of each scute on the carapace might become significantly raised as, beneath the carapace, keratin is added over the whole surface. It appears that the Malpighian cells are most active around the perimeter of each scute, so that the deposition of keratin here is greater than in the centre, known as the areola. In the case of captive-bred tortoises in particular, however, this natural imbalance in keratin production can be disturbed. Young chelonians growing at a fast rate, and being offered a diet high in protein, appear most at risk. This causes the individual scutes to develop a domed shape, rather than keeping a relatively even profile.

The outer keratin covering of the carapace can become worn, most obviously in burrowing species, such as the *Gopherus* tortoises, giving a smooth surface to the shell. Some aquatic chelonians, such as the red-eared slider, actually shed their scutes as they grow, and so no accumulation of growth rings is visible on their shells. The old scutes start to loosen from around their edges towards the centre, and can later be found as translucent rubbery scales in the water. It has been suggested that basking is important to ensure the successful shedding of the scutes, and that if they are not shed, subsequent growth abnormalities of the shell may then result.

The bony shell

The bony plates of young chelonians are usually not fused on hatching, but gradually grow together, joining in a zig-zag pattern of sutures. From this stage onwards, growth of the overall shell slows down, although new bone may continue to be deposited around the perimeters of the plates. When the sutures themselves become completely ossified, the shell has reached its maximum size.

Modifications to the bony plates are seen in some species, which have developed hinges over the surfaces of their shells. The formation of a hinge depends upon the spread of cartilaginous tissue between the sutures of the particular bony plates. Certain species have evolved more than one hinge, as in the case of the *Cuora* box turtles from south-eastern parts of Asia, extending into China. In this case, hinges at both ends of the plastron enable these chelonians to seal themselves totally within

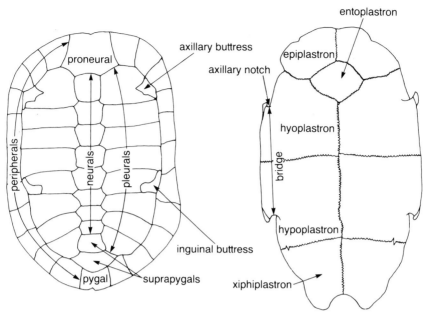

Fig. 3 The typical arrangement of the bony plates, again showing both dorsal and ventral views.

their shells when threatened. The hingeback tortoises, occurring through much of Africa south of the Sahara, have developed a slightly different method of protection, with a rear hinge set into their carapaces, so that their hindquarters are fully protected. It is said that, when they are

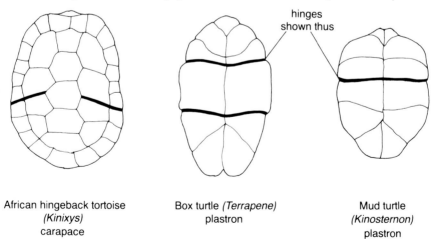

African hingeback tortoise
(Kinixys)
carapace

Box turtle *(Terrapene)*
plastron

Mud turtle
(Kinosternon)
plastron

Fig. 4 Hinges provide an additional means of protection, enabling the chelonian to retreat to a greater extent within its shell. Here are three examples of the positions of hinges within the overall shell structure.

Plate 8 In some species, such as the North American box turtle (*Terrapene* spp) shown here, the shell has been modified so that the chelonian can withdraw completely when threatened. Cartilaginous attachments enable the reptile to close hinges at the front and rear of the plastron.

resting, these tortoises partially bury themselves, their protected rear legs being covered by the shell.

A reduction in the bony body-casing is seen in another African species, the pancake tortoise (*Malacochersus tornieri*). This tortoise relies on speed, and its flattened shape, rather than a heavy domed shell, to escape predators in its rocky environment. The soft-shelled turtles of the family Trionychidae also show a similar reduction in the bony layer of

Plate 9 In the pancake tortoise (*Malacochersus tornieri*), the shell has become lightened by a reduction in the bony plates, and flattened in shape. This enables these tortoises to escape quickly when threatened, and to hide under low rocks.

Plate 10 Several species of tortoises have an attractively marked shell, as shown here by the leopard tortoise (*Geochelone pardalis*). The markings can vary quite widely between individuals, with the pattern forming as the tortoise grows.

as albinism, is a rare, but not unknown feature in chelonians. A number of albino common snapping turtles have been recorded from various North American localities, ranging from Canada south to Florida. A captive breeding pair of *Trachemys (scripta) dorbignyi* in Argentina have successfully produced similarly coloured offspring, and it is likely that, as with other reptiles, study would reveal that such mutations were of the autosomal recessive type in terms of their mode of inheritance.

Albino tortoises are also known, including a desert tortoise (*Gopherus agassizii*) and a Hermann's tortoise (*Testudo hermanni*). Loggerhead and green turtles (*Caretta caretta* and *Chelonia mydas*) lacking pigment have similarly been recorded. Partial loss of colour pigment has also been observed in the green turtle. Chelonians affected in this way are liable to be at a disadvantage in the wild, being more conspicuous to potential predators. They are, therefore, less likely to survive to reproduce successfully, transmitting the mutation to the next generation in the process. With the exception of *Trachemys (scripta) dorbignyi*, there appears to have been no real success in establishing these colour variants by means of captive breeding, in contrast to the situation with snakes, and they remain very rare. In some cases further study may reveal that the colour aberration itself is not always of genetic origin, but could result from environmental factors.

Plate 13   Shell damage in chelonians is not uncommon, and will heal, but the process is slow. In this instance, part of the bony layer has been forced out and is protruding through the surrounding keratin. Note the zig-zag suture pattern, which is not normally visible.

Shell damage

Injury to the shell is not uncommon, especially in certain localities. Tortoises are at risk from agricultural machinery and can be crushed in rocky areas. The extent of injury is very variable. In some cases, the bone beneath the scutes may be fractured. But even if the bony casing is punctured, there is no interference with the respiratory process, as happens in mammals which suffer a deep chest wound of this type. This is because the chest area is not maintained at positive pressure, nor indeed is there a diaphragm within the chelonian's body. Their lungs will not collapse once the cavity is punctured, so this type of injury is not as serious as in mammals.

Surgical repair of the shell is frequently carried out successfully in captive chelonians, following radiography to establish the extent of the injury. Treatment consists of lifting compacted bone fragments back to their approximate position, and then applying a small amount of a polymer to the top of each piece. This will serve to anchor the pieces together, with each one then being attached to an overlying fibreglass patch. A variety of products have been used successfully for polymerisation purposes. Those which do not produce much heat when the polymer is being formed are favoured by veterinarians working in this field.

Plate 14   Here the damage is more superficial, and does not involve the bony layer beneath. In some cases following injury to the shell, there may be accompanying haemorrhage. An injury of this type may result from a fall, while damage to the keratin can also be caused by fire. Terrestrial species are most at risk.

The fibreglass is itself fixed in turn to the outer surface of the cara-pace, clear of the wound. It holds all the fragments in position, so that the broken pieces of bone can fuse back together, unimpaired around the edges. The bony casing should then be restored, and keratin deposition may then follow on top, but healing in chelonians is a slow process, and this is likely to take between one and two years. In young animals, the supporting bridge will need to be removed, at least in part, after about six months, so that normal growth can continue unchecked. If the resin actually becomes stuck between the bony fragments rather than on top of them, this will prevent healing. In more severe cases, however, where the bone cannot be repaired, it is possible to construct a replacement section of shell by similar means, after careful cleaning of the site.

Fire clearly represents a hazard to a slow-moving creature such as a tortoise, although the shell again provides some protection. In typically arid areas, such as parts of Africa, where bush fires occur regularly, the flames tend to pass rapidly over the ground and cause little physical injury to tortoises in their path. Traditionally, however, rubbish dumps are a favoured site for hibernation in the case of pet tortoises in Europe. Here chelonians are much more vulnerable to the effects of fire, because their metabolism, and thus their movement, are slowed at this time of year. In such cases, the keratin covering over the shell is liable to be permanently damaged, and the growth rings will be lost – assuming that the chelonian can escape the flames at all. If the Malpighian layer is destroyed, the keratin will not be replaced, but the reptile may survive. The situation is obviously more critical if the soft tissue of the body is injured.

Burrowing chelonians are also at risk from shell damage, as, especially during hibernation, the scutes may be attacked by various invertebrates present in the soil. This results in a pitted surface, most notably along the plastron. Such signs are more common in certain species, especially those which inhabit damp terrain, such as the *Terrapene* box turtles. In severe cases, the invertebrates may actually burrow down into the bony plates beneath the scutes, and although some regeneration is possible, the chelonian is likely to be permanently scarred.

A developmental weakness, which dramatically alters the appearance of the shell, is kyphosis. It is most commonly encountered in soft-shelled turtles (Trionychidae), and results in a hump-backed carapace. The cause is unclear, but probably results, at least in part, from an abnor-mally large yolk sac, which alters the growth pattern of the embryonic chelonian. The carapace becomes excessively curved, and this may lead to an early union of the ribs and bony plates, prior to hatching. As the vertebrae normally grow more rapidly than the plates at this stage, expanding the gaps between the ribs, this will inevitably lead to the carapace itself developing a humped appearance.

Bone structure

The vertebral column of chelonians is greatly modified. They possess eight cervical vertebrae, which are extremely flexible, compared with the seven bones present in the vertebral columns of the vast majority of mammals. Also in contrast, the central part of the vertebral column has become fused to act as a support for the carapace, being joined to the neural bones of the shell. The number of vertebrae has been reduced to ten in this section, while the tail comprises up to 33 bones, and, like the neck, is quite flexible. When threatened, a chelonian will often withdraw its tail, curling it back tightly against the rear of its body.

The ribs attached to the ten dorsal vertebrae are arranged in an unusual fashion when compared with the limb girdles, and actually envelope them. The reason for this distinctive growth pattern can be found during the embryonic phase of development. The early carapace, described as the anlage, first appears at a point in the middle of the back, and grows out from here, rather like a sheet. Just beneath the anlage, the ribs are also forming, but at a slower rate, and so they are

Plate 15   A view of the inner surface of a chelonian's carapace. The attachment of the vertebral column can be clearly seen in the midline. Considerable modifications to the skeletal system have occurred, enabling it to become largely encased in the shell.

29

Plate 16   The Chinese big-headed turtle (*Platysternon megacephalum*) is an agile species, which may seek refuge in trees when out of the water, using its claws for climbing. Its long tail may help it to retain its balance.

effectively shaped by the anlage above. The ribs, therefore, also develop in a relatively horizontal position, and come to encase the limb girdles. In fact, the overall growth of the embryo tends to be much greater in the horizontal rather than the vertical plane.

The limb bones have also undergone significant modification. For example, the collar bone, or clavicle, is represented as a plastral component, in the form of a bony plate known as the epiplastron. The shoulder blade, or scapula, has become joined to the carapace by its outer surface, which serves to anchor the fore limbs more effectively in position. The normally protective breastbone, or sternum, appears to have been totally lost, serving no useful function in the rigidly encased chelonian.

Both the humerus and the femur have become shortened in the chelonian's fore and hind limbs, but, conversely, these bones are enlarged at the ends. This is because they are being used to support the weight-bearing joints, being positioned in a horizontal plane. Further down the limbs, fusion of both carpal and tarsal elements is evident, strengthening the distal parts of the legs.

The fore limb itself usually terminates in five digits, with attached claws. Exceptions to this basic pattern are not unknown. Horsfield's tortoise (*Testudo horsfieldii*), for example, lacks the fourth digit. In the case of the hind limbs, the fifth digit is usually reduced in all species, except in the helmeted turtle (*Pelomedusa subrufa*) which maintains five digits on all its feet.

The claws may be used for climbing, as in the big-headed turtle (*Platysternon megacephalum*), or burrowing, as shown by the gopher tortoises (*Gopherus* spp). The feet of the fore limbs of this particular group are also strengthened to assist in excavations. Gophers may tunnel at least 9 m (30 ft) underground, and also walk directly on their claws, unlike other species.

The feet of aquatic chelonians show signs of webbing between the toes, in contrast to their terrestrial counterparts. Within the family Emydidae, this is clearly visible in *Trachemys* species, but the related box turtles (*Terrapene* spp), which spend the majority of their time on land, have feet resembling those of tortoises.

In aquatic chelonians, the claws can provide a means of sexing in some cases, and are used for display purposes. Male red-eared sliders (*T. scripta elegans*) have relatively long claws on their front feet, and fan these

Plate 17   The structure of the feet of chelonians differs considerably, and directly reflects their lifestyle. Here, the webbing reveals a highly aquatic species, the linkage between the toes assisting with propulsion through the water.

31

Plate 18   The long claws seen in the case of this red-eared slider (*Trachemys scripta elegans*) are not a deformity, but a secondary sexual characteristic, used for gripping the edge of the female's shell during mating.

in front of a female as a prelude to mating. The most aquatic species, including the soft-shelled turtles (Trionychidae) and cheloniids, have rigid toes. They also show a reduction in the number of claws, ranging from three in the case of the soft-shells, to a total absence of claws on the feet of the leatherback turtle (*Dermochelys coriacea*). The cheloniids retain just one claw, with a vestigial second usually also visible.

The digestive system

The modern chelonian lacks teeth of any kind, relying instead on the sharp cutting edges of its horny jaws to tear its food. The front feet also have a role to play in this respect. Aquatic species often use their feet in conjunction with their jaws, anchoring the food in their mouths and then pushing the surplus away with feet and claws. In contrast, the two *Cyclemys* species, especially *C. mouhoti*, a semi-terrestrial emydid, actually use the upper surface of their forefeet rather like hands. They can transfer food directly to their mouths by this means. Tortoises tend to stand on top of vegetation, using their forefeet to anchor the plant down firmly, so that the shoots can be nibbled off more easily.

Soft-shells are unusual amongst chelonians, as, rather than having obvious horny jaws, the lips are covered with flesh. They do not seem to suffer from the malformation of the mouthparts, caused by excessive keratin overgrowth, seen in other species, notably tortoises and semi-terrestrial chelonians. The degree of distortion is variable, and may be influenced by diet. Ripe fruits exert little wear on the mouthparts, compared with fibrous greenstuff.

Plate 19   Chelonians lack teeth, but rely on sharp powerful jaws to cut and tear their food into suitable pieces which can be swallowed. Their front feet may also be used for this purpose. Terrestrial species tend to be far less carnivorous than their aquatic counterparts.

Plate 20 The sense of smell is very important to a chelonian seeking food. The Mediterranean spur-thighed tortoise (*Testudo graeca*) shown here, like other species, will pause to sniff a potential food item before deciding to eat it.

Within the mouth, the thick vascular tongue, anchored quite rigidly to the floor, serves to direct food down the gullet. The digestive tract itself is adapted to the feeding habits of each particular species and, not surprisingly, the intestines of primarily herbivorous species are greatly elongated, to cope with large quantities of fibre being ingested. They can be up to seven times longer than the shell itself, with the domed carapace of tortoises helping to accommodate this additional bulk. The actual structure of the tract is, surprisingly, not very specialised, and there is no equivalent 'fermentation chamber', such as the rumen of many mammalian herbivores, to facilitate the breakdown of plant cellulose by micro-organisms, so that it can be absorbed.

The food intake of chelonians can be influenced both by age and availability, with many species altering their diet through the year. Members of the genera *Chrysemys* and *Trachemys* both tend to switch from a carnivorous to a more omnivorous diet as they get older, even becoming largely vegetarian later in life. This is almost certainly a reflection of their changing nutritional requirements, from their major growth phase through to adulthood. Similar changes have been observed in the case of sea turtles, with hatchling green turtles (*Chelonia mydas*) being omnivorous at first. Only when they weigh around 22 kg (10 lb) will they switch to a primarily herbivorous diet.

Seasonal changes can also be observed, especially in temperate zones, when live food is available in abundance. During the warmer parts of the year, for example, mud turtles (*Kinosternon* spp) feed predominantly on insects and similar items, reverting to plants and berries to sustain them throughout the winter. Food intake is temperature-dependent, and most

34

Plate 21   The unusual fleshy lips of the Malayan soft-shell (*Trionyx subplanus*) can be clearly seen in this photograph. Most chelonians have sharp edges to their jaws, which can sometimes become malformed. Tortoises feeding on a diet of fruit over a period of time may develop a horny overgrowth, typically creating the appearance of a beak.

Plate 22   The scorpion mud turtle (*Kinosternon scorpioides*) is an opportunist feeder, taking a variety of foods through the year. It will feed predominantly on live food when available, in preference to plant matter.

species will stop feeding outside the range of 20–32°C (68–90°F). The leatherback turtle (*Dermochelys coriacea*) is known to feed when the sea is at a much lower temperature, around 12°C (57°F), but this species is capable of maintaining its own temperature at a higher level than that of its environment.

The time taken for food to pass through the digestive tract is also influenced by the environmental temperature. Indeed, people are usually recommended not to feed *Testudo* species, popular as pets, for several weeks prior to hibernation, for fear that the food may actually putrify in the gut. Digestion and absorption cease once the temperature falls to 6°C (43°F). Studies with barium meals, followed by radiography, have shown that food material normally remains in the tract for nearly four weeks. Even where gut motility is greatly increased, in tortoises with severe diarrhoea, a period of at least five days will elapse before excretion occurs.

The combination of the greatly elongated intestinal tract and the slow rate of passage ensures that tortoises can obtain maximum nutritional benefit from their food, in the absence of any specialised digestive facilities. It is believed that up to 30 per cent of the cellulose ingested is actually broken down during its passage through the gut. Commensal bacteria and other micro-organisms are almost certainly vital to this task, but further study of their involvement is still to be carried out. It seems likely that they are concentrated in the lower part of the digestive tract, with breakdown of other foods occurring under enzymatic influence in the small, rather than the large intestine.

Absorbed foodstuffs surplus to the body's energy and growth requirements are likely to be converted to fat. Unlike the situation in mammals, however, chelonians do not have subcutaneous fat stores just beneath the skin. This sort of fat provides insulation and could, therefore, presumably interfere with the thermo-regulatory mechanisms of creatures which are primarily ectothermic. Instead, fat is stored within the abdomen, in lumps described as fat bodies. These tend to become most conspicuous in the autumn, probably under hormonal influence, and provide a means of sustaining chelonians through a period of hibernation, or certainly one of reduced activity, until the following spring, in temperate areas.

The actual energy requirement of these reptiles is surprisingly low. One study revealed that a red-footed tortoise (*Geochelone carbonaria*) weighing 4.3 kg (9½ lb), with a shell length of nearly 30 cm (12 in), only required 185 g (6½ oz) of banana to meet its energy needs for about four weeks when kept at a temperature of 17°C (63°F). There is no doubt that chelonians can survive for considerable periods without eating, possibly for a year in some species, provided that their fat stores are adequate in the first instance. Hatchlings also possess food reserves, in the remains of their yolk sacs, and will not starve if they cannot feed immediately on emerging from the eggs. A chelonian which refuses food over several months is actually more at risk from succumbing to an infection, being in a debilitated and often dehydrated state, before its fat stores are exhausted.

It is at the end of the digestive system where the most significant distinction between the anatomy of the reptilian and mammalian tracts is apparent. Instead of a rectum, chelonians possess a cloaca. This is a vital meeting point, through which both faecal matter from the gut and urinary waste from the kidneys are voided. In addition, the respective genital openings are situated in the cloaca, and are connected to the outside world via the anus, visible towards the base of the tail.

Urinary output

The kidneys of chelonians are remarkably adapted to meet the needs of the particular species concerned. In the case of fresh-water turtles, there is little need to worry about conservation of water, in direct contrast to the situation for desert-dwelling tortoises, such as the desert tortoise (*Gopherus agassizii*). As a result, highly aquatic turtles, such as the green turtle (*Chelonia mydas*), are able to void toxic ammonia directly in a pure form, simply by flushing it out of their bodies. More terrestrial species must convert this chemical to urea, a somewhat less toxic form, which can be eliminated with a lower fluid requirement. Tortoises, in contrast, produce uric acid as the main means of excreting nitrogenous waste from their bodies, with water conservation being of prime concern. Uric acid is a concentrated, yet safe, form of the by-products of body metabolism, being voided as a whitish, semi-solid material.

The actual proportions of uric acid and urea excreted do vary, however, and are probably influenced, at least to some extent, by the availability of water. The actual mechanisms involved in determining fluctuations are not entirely clear, and may differ according to individual species of tortoise. It has been suggested that urea present in the cloaca can be reabsorbed and then converted into uric acid. Significant variations in the relative output of these two chemicals have been observed in several species, whereas in others, such as the starred tortoise (*Geochelone elegans*), the proportions remain quite constant, with only about 20 per cent being excreted as urea.

Water storage and conservation

Chelonians are able to store water within their bodies, with water and accompanying salts being passed back from the cloaca to the bladder and also to the colon in the large intestine. This means that fluid which would otherwise have been lost can be drawn back into the body. The bladder itself, in tortoises, is a particularly valuable site for the storage of water, a fact soon appreciated by sailors visiting the Galapagos, who found giant tortoises here. Living on islands a significant distance from the mainland, these beasts could provide not only fresh meat, but also an invaluable supply of potable water for the seamen.

Some chelonians also possess cloacal bladders, which may occur in pairs. These are located close to the anal opening, and are frequently emptied without warning if the tortoise is handled. They would appear

37

Plate 23   The ability of chelonians to survive for long periods without food and water was exploited by sailors who discovered the giant populations on the Galapagos and Aldabran Islands. They kept these reptiles on board ship for months, to provide a ready supply of fresh meat.

Plate 24   Tortoises, such as the gopher species (*Gopherus*), are well able to survive in areas where water is in short supply. They are able to extract fluid from plant matter, and can restrict water loss from their bodies to a minimum.

to provide an auxiliary means of storing water in the body, but are not present in all species.

Tortoises can survive quite adequately for long periods without drinking, obtaining fluid from the plant matter on which they feed. Water may also be produced directly as a result of metabolic pathways, in the case of omnivorous species, and again this occurs irrespective of fluid intake. Terrestrial chelonians will drink considerable volumes of water when this is available, to replenish their body stores. A study of the desert tortoise (*Gopherus agassizii*) revealed that this species would drink over 40 per cent of its body weight when given free access to water, within the space of an hour or so.

The shell of the tortoise may also provide a means of meeting the fluid requirements of at least some species, typically those found in areas of low rainfall. For example, a burrowing tortoise, which emerges from a relatively cool locality below ground, may well trigger the formation of dew from the atmosphere onto its shell, and also within its respiratory system, when it inhales the warm, moist air. The shape of the carapace can favour run-off of the droplets of dew towards the head. Here the moisture can be swallowed, enabling the chelonian to survive without access to free drinking water. Similarly, droplets of dew on plants will be ingested with this food, adding to the reptile's overall fluid intake.

In arid parts of Africa, where the run-off of rain is rapid, some tortoises appear to have evolved a means of catching the droplets directly, before they reach the ground, again using their shells for this purpose. Such behaviour has been observed in several species, including the tent tortoise (*Psammobates tentorius*). When the rains come, this South African species stands with its hind limbs raised, so that the droplets falling on the shell flow in the direction of its head. The water is retained in small gullies on both sides of the carapace, formed by the raised edges of the

Plate 25 Home's hingeback tortoise (*Kinixys homeana*) is able to channel rainwater towards its head for drinking purposes. When water is not available, it may bury itself below ground, emerging when the rains come.

marginal scutes. The forelegs are also extended flat, in such a way that the rainwater is deliberately channelled to run off the shell and into the mouth, from both sides of the nuchal scute.

Although the skin of tortoises is dry and resistant to water loss, some water gain via this route may be feasible, at least in certain species. Reptilian skin is unusual, as, when it is fully immersed in water, its permeability actually increases. Certain chelonians, notably the giant tortoises, readily wallow in mud hollows, where there may be a little free water. Water uptake through the skin may be possible under these circumstances, while the covering of mud gained in the process will also serve to deter the attentions of mosquitoes and other biting insects.

One of the most effective means of conserving water is to reduce urinary output, and certainly terrestrial chelonians are well adapted in this case. The maximum urinary production of a Mediterranean spur-thighed tortoise (*Testudo graeca*) appears to be in the range of just 1–2 ml per day, whereas the desert-dwelling spurred tortoise (*Geochelone sulcata*) may produce only 0.62 ml of urine on a daily basis. These figures fall still further when the tortoise is dehydrated.

Physical means of reducing water loss are also apparent in both the lifestyle and anatomy of chelonians. Burrowing, for example, helps to prevent the excessive fluid loss which would otherwise be necessary to curb a rise in body temperature in the case of chelonians living under hot semi-desert conditions. The hinged structure of the shell of semi-terrestrial emydids may, in addition to its obvious protective function, also serve to restrict water loss from the body. This, in turn, enables the emydids to move further afield from their aquatic environment.

Living in salt water

Whereas marine turtles are capable of surviving exclusively in the oceans, species inhabiting brackish waters, such as the diamondback terrapin (*Malaclemys terrapin*), require access to fresh water for drinking purposes. Marine turtles have adapted totally to their environment by means of special tear glands, which provide the major route of excreting surplus sodium and potassium from the body. These lacrymal glands supplement the role of the kidneys, which would otherwise be unable to cope with the increased burden of salt ingested both in food and directly in seawater. The functioning of these glands is under the hormonal influence of the adrenal cortex, ensuring that the turtle does not become dehydrated in salt water. The same mechanism also controls the excretion of salts via the kidneys, and ensures effective overall regulation.

Sea turtles can therefore ingest seawater and excrete the salts, notably via the lacrymal glands, so that they remain hydrated, thus in effect converting salt water to fresh water. Any dietary excess of potassium can also be excreted by the same route. In contrast, the diamondback terrapin, in salt water, cannot maintain its salt balance so effectively, and thus becomes dehydrated over a period, as a build-up of salt takes place within the body. Presumably their lacrymal glands are less efficient than

Plate 26 Sea turtles are specially adapted to survive in a marine environment. Salt from sea water is excreted via the lacrymal glands of the eyes, as well as from the kidneys, so that they do not become dehydrated.

those of marine species. Interestingly, however, it appears that some fresh-water chelonians can survive in brackish water without these glands, as shown by the populations of the Florida red-bellied turtle (*Pseudemys nelsoni*) and the Cuban slider (*T. decussata*) inhabiting brackish waters in southern Florida and Grand Cayman Island respectively. A similar adaptation presumably permits the Nile soft-shell (*Trionyx triunguis*) to have colonised an area off the coast of Turkey, where salinity levels are in excess of 38 parts per 1,000.

Thermo-regulation and basking behaviour

The activity levels of chelonians are influenced primarily by the environmental temperature. They are popularly regarded as being 'cold-blooded', but, in fact, their body temperature, traditionally based on cloacal measurements, can be in excess of that of their environment. As ectotherms, chelonians do not possess elaborate means of producing and maintaining their own body heat on a constant basis. With little subcutaneous fat, they would be poorly equipped for this task in any event. However, the size of many chelonians provides protection against an immediate change in body temperature, relative to that of the environment.

41

Plate 27 The common snapping turtle (*Chelydra serpentina*) can remain active when the water temperature falls as low as 6°C (43°F). At this temperature, other chelonians would become torpid.

Chelonians regulate their body temperature largely by behavioural means. The individual species each have preferred body temperatures, with those inhabiting hot areas having a higher optimum than chelonians found in more temperate regions. The desert gopher tortoise (*Gopherus agassizii*), for example, displays average activity with a body temperature around 31°C (88°F), whereas the slider turtle (*Trachemys scripta*) has a preferred optimum of about 25°C (77°F). At the lower end of the range, the gophers become fairly static when their temperature falls to 15°C (59°F), whereas the *Trachemys scripta* is still active at 10°C (50°F). Snapping turtles (*Chelydra serpentina*) have one of the lowest thresholds, remaining active at temperatures as low as 6°C (43°F).

There is also an upper limit, known as the critical thermal maximum, around 41°C (106°F), at which point the chelonian is liable to die. It is for this reason that desert tortoises retire to their burrows when the sun is at its hottest, around midday, so they do not become overheated. Seasonal changes occur, so that when the average peak daily temperature is lower, the tortoise will stay above ground for longer periods through the day. It will gain heat not only directly from the sun's rays, but also by conduction, being in contact with the warm earth or rocks which have previously been heated by the sun. Land tortoises will display basking behaviour, although this is generally less conspicuous than in their aquatic relatives. They will seek an area of warm ground and extend their hind legs out behind their shells, maximising the area of contact with the ground itself.

Water temperature is more stable and therefore rises less quickly than that of air. Partly for this reason, turtles, both marine and fresh-water, will choose to bask at the surface for short periods. This behaviour is most common in members of the family Emydidae. Apart from increasing their body temperature, however, there are other benefits to be gained by basking. Sunlight contains ultra-violet rays, and these trigger the synthesis of vitamin D_3, which has a crucial role to play in the organisa-

Plate 28   Members of the slider (*Trachemys*) genus, although primarily aquatic by nature, regularly bask out of the water. This enables them to synthesise vitamin D_3 essential for a healthy skeleton, and often raises their body temperature above that of the water.

Plate 29   When basking, turtles remain alert to any hint of danger, and will scuttle back into the water if they are threatened in any way. Basking can also assist in the shedding of shell scutes, and can help to prevent algal colonisation of the shell, a particular problem in sluggish stretches of water.

tion of the body's stores of calcium and phosphorus. A shortage of this vitamin causes the condition known as softshell, recognised in captive turtles kept indoors without access to sunlight or to artificial sources of this vitamin. A weakening of the limbs, and a softening of the bony shell are characteristic features.

Basking on land also enables the aquatic chelonian to dry its body, and this may help to control potential pathogens, such as fungi. It certainly assists in the shedding of shell scutes, and could restrict algal growth on the shell. In some cases this can become a problem, with the algae actually penetrating between the scutes.

Working with laboratory models, the shape of the carapace has been shown to exert an effect on the rate of heat gain. Flat-shelled chelonians, such as the Florida soft-shell (*Trionyx ferox*), show a more rapid increase in body temperature than those with domed carapaces, such as the musk turtles (*Sternotherus* spp). The shell surface itself tends to act as an insulating layer, creating a temperature differential between here and the body beneath. Other factors, apart from shape, can also influence the absorption of radiated heat, such as the colour of the carapace. Pale scutes may actually slow down the rate of solar gain, because of their increased reflective abilities, compared with a dark-coloured carapace.

Apart from sunlight, wind speed is another factor which exerts an influence on basking behaviour. It tends to limit and lower the increase in body temperature which can be anticipated, and also causes more rapid dehydration. Indeed, turtles are generally less keen to bask in windy conditions, irrespective of the degree of cloud cover.

Aquatic chelonians are capable of gaining heat much more rapidly than they lose it, ensuring that they can derive the maximum thermo-regulatory benefit from basking in a relatively short space of time. This is achieved by alterations in the pattern of blood flow to the skin and carapace. Conversely, some species, such as the Florida gopher tortoise, may cool down faster, which is clearly advantageous if there is a risk of exceeding the critical thermal maximum. Aquatic species can simply return to the water, which will be cooler, once they have attained their optimum temperature.

Tortoises are less likely to be able to immerse themselves in water in order to cool down. They rely instead on using body fluids, evaporated from the skin surface, for this purpose. In the case of the common box turtle (*Terrapene carolina*) for example, salivation occurs when the animal's body temperature rises to about 32°C (90°F). This is then smeared over the legs, and onto the head. Cooling of the hind limbs is achieved by urination, and the fluid present in the bladder may also be used for this purpose. A discharge from the eyes is also evident in some species, with fluid running down over the face. The rate of respiration also rises, with the resultant evaporation of water serving to lower the body temperature.

These means of thermo-regulation are relatively primitive, although one species of chelonian, the leatherback turtle (*Dermochelys coriacea*), appears to have a limited ability to control its body temperature more effectively, independent of its environment. A temperature difference of

Plate 30 Soft-shell turtles have a relatively flat shell, even amongst aquatic chelonians, which are more streamlined than their terrestrial relatives, and this can speed up a rise in body temperature when they are exposed to sunlight.

Plate 31 Opening of the mouth, as shown by this European pond turtle (*Emys orbicularis*), is a common gesture when a chelonian starts to move again after a period of inactivity, or prior to eating.

Plate 32 Turtles shed skin from their bodies, but this comes off in small pieces, rather than as lumps. Scratching with the legs can help to facilitate the shedding process.

as much as 18°C (66°F), between the turtle and the sea water in which it is kept, has been measured. The turtle can effectively maintain its body temperature at 25.5°C (78°F) under these conditions.

This is accomplished in several ways. First, the leatherback is unusual in possessing a thick layer of fat, which serves to insulate its body, preventing heat loss via the skin. In the wild, the species often wanders into cold northern waters, being seen off the coasts of Britain and parts of America where the temperature has been measured at only 12°C (54°F). Further restriction of heat loss is made possible by the presence of a vascular counter-current exchange system in the limbs of these turtles. This enables transference of heat to take place between the arterial and venous circulations. It is achieved by having the vessels in close contact, with heat passing directly from the warmer arterial blood back to the colder venous blood which is returning to the centre of the body.

A study of other sea turtles has revealed less effective means of temperature control. They do appear able to increase their body temperature slightly, however, as when diving into deeper, colder water. Their average body temperature tends to be about 3°C (5°F) above that of their environment under these circumstances. Undoubtedly, the relatively large body size of marine turtles also helps them to maintain their inner body temperature.

Hibernation

As the environmental temperature falls, chelonians enter a state of dormancy, often described as hibernation, although the accompanying physiological changes seen in mammals in this state do not appear to occur. Reptiles, for example, are not able to shiver. In addition, such periods of dormancy are not necessarily triggered by a decline in temperature; food availability is also significant. In Africa, for example, Bell's hingeback tortoise (*Kinixys belliana*) is known to bury itself during prolonged periods of drought, emerging at the onset of the rains.

47

Studies involving the *Testudo* species commonly kept as pets have revealed some interesting facts about their hibernating behaviour in the wild. In Morocco, spur-thighed tortoises (*T. graeca*) have been discovered hibernating as early as August. The length of time spent hibernating depends on local environmental factors. Observations on populations of Horsfield's tortoise (*Testudo (Agrionemys) horsfieldii*), in Kazakhstan, USSR, have revealed that here this species is only active for about three months of the year, from the end of March to the middle of June. For the remainder of the year these tortoises remain buried underground, occasionally emerging again for a brief period at the end of the summer.

Indeed, it is now clear that chelonians do not hibernate for a set period of time. They may re-emerge when conditions are favourable, in order to feed and build up their fat stores. Aquatic species will bury themselves in the bottoms of ponds. With their body processes slowed down, so that their oxygen requirement is reduced, they are likely to sustain themselves by means of gaseous exchange with the water during

Plate 33   Chelonians found in temperate areas, such as the map turtles (*Graptemys* spp) are likely to undergo an annual period of hibernation in the winter. Such physiological changes will be influenced by the pineal body in the brain.

Plate 34 A typical European habitat for turtles. This is the Rio Sado, near Alentejo in Portugal. It is a relatively slow-flowing stretch of water, with waterweed and small areas of land in the river itself where turtles can bask, largely unmolested.

this period. Marine turtles may also undergo seasonal periods of inactivity, similar to those of their fresh-water counterparts.

Breathing

The shell of the chelonian places immediate strictures on the respiratory process, because the ribs are fixed to the shell. The muscles which control breathing open into the limb pockets at the borders of the shell, and thus serve to modify the internal pressure within a chelonian's body. It used to be thought that there was, here, a parallel with amphibians, in that the obvious throat movements of chelonians, described as gular pumping, were responsible for drawing air, under positive pressure, into

49

the lungs. This movement is now known to be of olfactory significance only in chelonians. Respiration occurs by the creation of negative pressure in the lungs. Inspiration takes place as a result of the pressure differential.

The degree of muscular activity required for this purpose is partially influenced by the shell. Species with a rigid shell, such as most tortoises, use their musculature both for inspiratory and expiratory movements. The situation differs somewhat for aquatic species, as in the case of the common snapping turtle (*Chelydra serpentina*). This species, and presumably others with a similarly reduced plastral area, is able to breathe on land with little effort, as the weight of its internal organs, under the influence of gravity, serves to draw air into the lungs which are located near the top of the shell. Expiration, in contrast, requires muscular effort.

Once the chelonian is actually in the water, however, the situation tends to be reversed, as its body is affected by water pressure. Inspiration depends on muscular involvement, whereas expiration, because of the presence of the surrounding water, takes place virtually spontaneously, although, in marine species especially, the depth of water is significant in this respect.

The volume of air in the lungs of aquatic species also clearly affects their buoyancy. It is no coincidence that chelonians with a relatively light shell, such as the soft-shells (Trionychidae), have small lungs compared with those that have a heavy shell. This undoubtedly helps to prevent them from sinking. Studies involving the red-eared slider (*Trachemys scripta elegans*) have revealed that in order to remain buoyant, about 14 per cent of its total body volume has to be air. The importance of the lungs as a buoyancy aid is evident when a turtle develops pneumonia. It is then unable to dive, and remains floating in the water at an abnormal angle.

Alterations in lung volume within the confines of the chelonian's shell must affect the other organs. It is now clear that there is a close relationship between the lung volume and the volume of the bladder and cloacal sacs. As lung volume increases, fluid is expelled from these body organs to compensate for this gain. The reverse occurs when the lung volume contracts, and this serves to maintain the chelonian's state of buoyancy.

The actual pattern of respiration varies according to the lifestyle of the chelonian. Land tortoises breathe in a fairly regular way, whereas aquatic species breathe rapidly when they come to the water's surface, and then cease to do so until they resurface again. They can, in fact, manage quite adequately for several hours without breathing. Musk turtles (*Sternotherus* spp) have survived in an atmosphere of pure nitrogen for half a day, whereas a mammal kept in these surroundings would die in minutes.

Aquatic chelonians do not rely exclusively on their lungs in order to obtain oxygen, and this means that they can remain under water for even longer periods than would otherwise be possible. When submerged,

Plate 35   The mata mata (*Chelus fimbriatus*), a South American species equipped with snorkel-like nostrils which enable it to lurk quietly for long periods in shallow water, ready to pounce on passing prey.

they are likely to be less vulnerable to predators. Some species, such as the mata mata (*Chelus fimbriatus*), which rely on camouflage to catch prey, can stay concealed for long periods. In common with the soft-shell turtles (Trionychidae), the nasal region of this species is elongated, enabling the nose to be used as a snorkel when the turtles are in shallow water.

The nostrils are also utilised, at least in some species, for breathing when they are under water. Certainly, the Australian species *Chelodina expansa* breathes in this way. A large species, growing to 40 cm (16 in), with a raised, heavy shell, these turtles tend to remain close to the bottom of the creeks where they live, often in water as much as 3.6 m (12 ft) in depth. Observations in aquarium surroundings have revealed that they suck in water through their nostrils, which is then retained in their mouths. After a period, the water is expelled from the mouth. Measurements of the oxygen level in the water have shown that during this period the turtles extract oxygen from the water. This is achieved by means of pharyngeal respiration. The pharyngeal area, at the back of the mouth, is highly vascularised, enabling gaseous exchange to take place here, with oxygen coming out of the water and entering the blood stream.

The method of pharyngeal respiration appears to differ according to the species concerned. In the case of the soft-shell genus *Trionyx*, for example, the water flow is reversed, with water entering the mouth and then being expelled from the nostrils. These turtles appear to be more dependent on pharyngeal respiration, maintaining a virtually constant water flow in this manner, in contrast to *Chelodina expansa*.

A similar additional means of respiration is achieved via the sacs in the cloaca. These thin-walled structures are also able to function as a gaseous exchange mechanism, and probably help to meet the oxygen requirements of chelonians hibernating in winter underwater. In this state, the turtles will remain submerged for weeks, until the water temperature increases during the spring. They are unaffected by the formation of ice on the surface of the water.

In addition to pharyngeal respiration, soft-shell turtles (Trionychidae) also rely on their shells for gaseous exchange. The blood supply just beneath the leathery skin is used for this purpose. This dependence on an aquatic supply of oxygen can, however, be hazardous. Soft-shells are acutely susceptible to the effects of dissolved poisons in their water. This was first noted when derris was used selectively to poison lakes in Florida in order to carry out population studies on fish. The active ingredient of derris, rotenone, is known to be a respiratory poison and, as well as fish, soft-shelled turtles also succumbed in these lakes. Other aquatic chelonians were not affected.

The circulatory system

The chelonian heart comprises only three chambers, although a partial septum is present within the ventricle. This means that oxygenated blood from the lungs, leaving the heart, also contains some venous blood which has been returned from the peripheral circulation via the right atrium. The amount of mixing is minimal because of pressure differentials under normal circumstances. However, during diving, the degree of mixing increases as pulmonary resistance rises. The situation is then reversed when the chelonian returns to the surface where gaseous exchange via the lungs takes place.

The heart rate itself is influenced by various factors, including temperature. A rise in temperature triggers an increase in heart rate, which is further emphasised by activity. The reverse situation occurs when the chelonian dives, and a noticeable reduction, termed bradycardia, is detectable. This prepares the chelonian for a period of submergence underwater.

Oxygen in the blood is carried in association with haemoglobin, and two distinct forms can be distinguished. There is an embryonic form, which, at least in the case of the diamondback terrapin (*Malaclemys terrapin*), can be detected in the circulation of individuals up to two years old. This may be a reflection of changes in the properties of haemoglobin once the chelonian enters water, after leaving the egg. Study of the oxygen-binding capacities of haemoglobin from various species reveal a distinct difference between that of terrestrial chelonians and their aquatic counterparts.

In the case of species which remain submerged for long periods, oxygen is released into the tissues quite readily, compared with the situation prevailing in tortoises. Not surprisingly, aquatic chelonians can carry high levels of carbon dioxide in their blood, and this helps to protect them from the effects of metabolic acidosis. There are also likely to be differences in blood chemistry between the more active aquatic chelonians and those which are essentially sedentary, such as the mata mata (*Chelus fimbriatus*). Marine turtles have an even greater tendency to absorb oxygen into their bodies from their blood than fresh-water species.

When the turtle dives, a number of significant physiological changes occur. The level of oxygen in the blood falls, as this is liberated to the body tissues. Anaerobic metabolism, which does not require oxygen, gradually predominates, causing a build-up of lactic acid, and carbon dioxide levels also rise. On their return to the water's surface, however, turtles are able to reverse these changes very rapidly. This is achieved by means of hyperventilation when atmospheric oxygen is available. The rate of breathing may increase to nearly ten times the level prior to diving. This, coupled with the reptile's ability to empty its lungs almost totally when breathing, ensures that the level of oxygen in the blood is rapidly restored. Other changes, such as the relative acidity of the blood, take longer to reverse, but with its oxygen level raised, the turtle can dive again as necessary.

One significant anomaly in the diving physiology has yet to be fully explained and, at first sight, appears irreconcilable. The turtle breathes in atmospheric air, full of oxygen, at the surface, and then dives, but, in so doing, the internal pressure is altered, re-routing deoxygenated blood away from the pulmonary circulation and out, via the ventricle, back into the arterial supply. This effectively leaves the oxygen supply untapped within the lungs.

It may be that extra-pulmonary respiration is of greater significance at this stage, as a supply of oxygen in solution is constantly available, and that the air in the lungs is of prime importance as a buoyancy aid, rather than to meet the turtle's oxygen requirements. Furthermore, the temperature of water falls as depth increases and in colder surroundings, the metabolic demands for oxygen also decline. In addition, carbon dioxide can be expelled efficiently from the body by means of extra-pulmonary respiration. The increased significance of this system is clearly evident in marine turtles (as well as soft-shells) which have evolved ribbons of tissue in the pharyngeal region. These serve to increase the surface area available here for oxygen uptake and gaseous exchange.

Lymphatics

The lymphatic system of chelonians is highly developed, although it appears that only one species, the common snapping turtle (*Chelydra serpentina*), actually has lymph nodes in its body. This species also has a mass of lymphatic tissue, apparently analogous to the avian bursa of Fabricius, present in its cloaca.

The actual production of antibodies in chelonians is known to be influenced by temperature. Living at a sub-optimal temperature will handicap a chelonian in combating an infection. Indeed, it is usually recommended that the environmental temperature is raised for a sick captive chelonian, as this can definitely enhance its chances of recovery. A decline in antibody production could be a factor in the increase in mortality usually encountered around or during hibernation. At this time, the reptile will be more vulnerable to infections, as its environmental temperature will have fallen.

Lymph follicles are most prominent in the vicinity of the digestive tract and spleen. Muscular movement of lymph is achieved by dilatations, known as lymph hearts, present in the larger vessels. From these, the lymph drains into the venous system. Apart from lymphocytes, other members of the white blood cell group can be identified in chelonian blood. They are, in fact, more numerous than those of mammals, but seasonal variations in their relative proportions have been detected. Lymphocytes predominate, certainly in species from temperate areas, during the summer months, while eosinophils are most common in the winter. This may be a reflection of an increasing parasitic burden at this stage.

The red blood cell population also changes through the year, building to a peak before the onset of hibernation, then falling during the following winter. This is one reason why chelonians that have recently emerged from hibernation may appear lethargic, as they are, in fact, anaemic.

After an injury which results in bleeding, clotting time is relatively prolonged, and this may be in part a reflection of the slow blood flow. Additionally, there is a potent natural anti-coagulatory compound present in chelonian blood, which handicaps external clotting. Chelonians are not usually exposed to the wounds associated with mammals, for example those caused by territorial or breeding behaviour, although, occasionally, a male may inflict injury on an intended mate.

Plate 36 The big-headed turtle (*Platysternon megacephalum*) cannot retract its head fully into its shell. As a result, this part of the body is well protected by a solid bony roof, covering the brain.

The brain and sensory systems

The brain of a chelonian reveals much about the development of its senses. Those parts concerned with sight and smell are clearly well developed. Interestingly, the area known as the pineal body, which forms the inner body clock, responding to changes in day length, and also of hormonal significance, is relatively large as well. This may well be important in determining the onset of hibernation as the days shorten, prior to the onset of winter in temperate areas.

The skull, housing the brain, offers solid protection to this vulnerable part of the chelonian's anatomy. The brain cavity in species such as the big-headed turtle (*Platysternon megacephalum*), which cannot retract its head, is buried beneath the solid bony roof of the skull and the under-lying muscle layers. In other species, where again there are no temporal openings, the skull may narrow posteriorly, forming a crest in some cases, to which the muscles of the jaw attach, depending upon the group concerned. The effective erosion of the lower edges is only encountered in members of the sea turtle family, Cheloniidae.

In vertebrates generally, the brain is extremely sensitive to oxygen deprivation, leading to irreversible changes which are disastrous for the creature concerned. This factor is probably the limiting feature for remaining under water, in the case of marine mammals. The brain of turtles is noticeably different in this regard, however, and continues to function effectively even when there is no oxygen left either in the lungs or within the blood. Nevertheless, some priority is given to maintaining a continuing supply of oxygen to the brain from the lungs after diving, at least in the loggerhead turtle (*Caretta caretta*).

Under normal circumstances, there is likely to be enough oxygen present for a short period underwater. The red blood cells are very effective in transporting oxygen from the lungs and yielding it into the body tissues. Only after about 20 minutes' submersion will the brain have to switch to anaerobic metabolism, as oxygen supplies are likely to be exhausted. Total replenishment of the oxygen stored in the lung can be accomplished by just three seconds at the water's surface. It now seems increasingly likely, therefore, that turtles are able to rely on oxygen to sustain brain activity when they dive, and only in unusual circumstances will they need to utilise the brain's ability to continue functioning, for at least several hours, in the absence of oxygen.

The vision of chelonians is highly developed. Sea turtles are able to see clearly through water, onto land. This is an important protective adaptation, as, once beached, turtles are extremely vulnerable to predators. Chelonians also possess colour vision, and this may explain why some species, notably tortoises, show colour preferences when feeding, favouring red and yellow items. The colour of the eyes themselves is a variable feature, tending to relatively dark in tortoises, and significantly brighter in many aquatic species. It appears that the irides blend in with the head markings, which are often yellow, as in the Amboina box turtle (*Cuora amboinensis*), and this disruptive coloration has a protective function. In one species, the common box turtle (*Terrapene carolina*), the coloration of the irides is indicative of sexual dimorphism. Males have bright reddish-orange irides, whereas those of females are dark brown in colour.

The eyes are protected in all species by heavy lids. An abnormality, resulting from a deficiency of vitamin A, seen most commonly in hatchling red-eared sliders (*Trachemys scripta elegans*) fed on a diet of raw meat, causes enlargement of the Harderian and lacrymal glands. This, in turn, leads to blindness, as the glands force the eyelids across the eyes. Affected chelonians do not feed, although, if corrected at an early stage, these effects can be reversed.

Chelonians also depend greatly on their sense of smell, both directly through the nose, and via Jacobsen's organ. This structure, found in the roof of the mouth, is connected directly to the brain, and serves to detect scent particles present in the air. It may also function under water, although it is not present in all species. The rigid tongue cannot assist in collecting molecules of scent, as in snakes, since it is firmly anchored to the floor of the mouth. The overall importance of scent to chelonians is reflected in the significant development of the olfactory bulbs in the brain.

Apart from indicating potential sources of food, it appears that scent plays an important role during the breeding season. In the elongated tortoise (*Geochelone elongata*), the blood flow to the nasal area increases, giving a pinkish colour to the skin. The local name for this species, '*laik nakhonga*', which translates as 'red-nosed tortoise', reflects this fact. A similar change is also evident in the closely related Travancore tortoise (*G. travancorica*).

The senses of sight and smell are, collectively, of great significance in determining food intake. There is some evidence to show that at least a few species possess taste buds as well. Snapping turtles (*Chelydra serpentina*) are said to have no such buds present on their tongues, and nor do some tortoises, but, overall, this aspect of chelonian physiology has not been well studied as yet. What is clear is that when feeding, irrespective of taste, tortoises can ingest poisonous plants, such as *Azalea*, in quantities that would prove toxic to mammalian herbivores, and yet apparently show no adverse effects in many cases.

Further evidence of the chelonian's dependence on olfactory stimuli is provided by the presence of external scent glands over the body surface. Their contents may be discharged when the turtle is threatened, with this means of defence being most obvious in the case of the stinkpot turtle (*Sternotherus odoratus*). Other members of the genus, collectively described as musk turtles, are also capable of producing a yellowish-coloured fluid from glands at both ends of the shell bridges, which is discharged through pores onto the skin's surface. Apart from providing an immediate deterrent to potential predators, the scent may also warn other chelonians, close at hand, of the perceived threat.

The scent liberated by the stinkpot is especially offensive to humans. Similar glands have been identified both in aquatic species, such as the common snapping turtle (*Chelydra serpentina*), and semi-terrestrial emydids, such as the box turtles (*Terrapene* spp). They are also present in the green turtle (*Chelonia mydas*), where the structure of the glands themselves is surprisingly similar, although, in this case, the secretion is whitish and virtually odourless to humans.

Turtles are actually able to use their olfactory senses while submerged, by adapting their throats for this purpose. This may involve Jacobsen's organ, if present in the mouth, with throat movements, or gular pumping, actively moving scent particles within the oral cavity.

Water drawn in through the nostrils may also pass via olfactory sensors, but many turtles keep their nasal passages closed under water. In order to exclude water from the lungs, the turtle also keeps its glottis closed, except when actually breathing. It is significant that olfactory movements are not detected at these times.

While chelonians are also sensitive to touch, in spite of their often thick shells, they are not well equipped to respond to auditory stimuli. They lack any external ear opening, although the tympanic membranes are clearly visible as patches covered by skin, on both sides of the head behind the eyes. Their auditory apparatus appears to be most responsive to low notes, in the frequency range of 60 to 100 Hz in the case of the green turtle (*Chelonia mydas*).

Chelonians are also generally quiet, and tend to vocalise only during the actual process of mating. Early writers often described the supposed calls of turtles, but it is likely that the sounds they heard resulted from involuntary grinding of shells, closing of jaws, or similar external contacts. Nevertheless, sea turtles are said to vocalise when injured, and, indeed, one of the traditional generic descriptions applied to the leatherback turtle, *Sphargis*, is derived from the Greek, meaning literally 'to make a noise'.

Behavioural intelligence

The popular image of the chelonian bestows an unusual degree of intelligence on these reptiles, stemming in part from their potential longevity. They certainly seem to possess a capability for memory, as the homing instincts of breeding sea turtles has confirmed. Terrestrial species can show a similar response when moved to an unfamiliar locality, even with barriers placed in their path. Leopard tortoises (*Geochelone pardalis*), moved up to 13 km (8 miles) from their usual range, returned to their original area of distribution within 14 days of being translocated.

Between them and their destination, they were faced with a fence of 7.5 cm (3 in) wire mesh, which was 1.2 m (4 ft) in height. When confronted with a solid barrier, such as a wall, chelonians may attempt to burrow underneath it, if they cannot reach over the top. Using their legs as supporting anchors, the tortoises apparently climbed this obstruction,

Plate 37   Clearly, any chelonian which is on its back is vulnerable to predators, and unless it can right itself, it will ultimately die. Sometimes, especially during the mating process, an individual may be tipped on to its carapace, but it can usually turn over again, using its muscular neck as well as its limbs for this purpose.

and presumably fell to the ground on the other side, righted themselves, and then continued on their journey. Some chelonians are more adept at climbing than others, and, generally, those with flatter shells, such as the pancake tortoise (*Malacochersus tornieri*), find it easier to turn over again if they fall onto their backs.

Although chelonians appear to have a distinct area, often described as the 'home range', where they are usually to be found, they are not territorial in the same way as most higher vertebrates. Variations in approach to other individuals in the area are most liable to be observed during the breeding period, although turtles generally tend not to be aggressive towards each other. It is significant, however, that species which do not have a full protective shell, such as a soft-shell turtle (Trionychidae) will attempt to bite, often without hesitation, when they are handled. Other chelonians, even if subjected to painful stimuli, will withdraw into their shells rather than respond in an aggressive manner.

The future

In spite of intensive study, both in the field and under laboratory conditions, much still remains to be learned about the biology of chelonians. Their basic lifestyles, with a few notable exceptions, have probably not altered significantly since the various groups evolved. Research efforts, however, have tended to concentrate largely on species which are readily available, such as the red-eared slider (*Trachemys scripta elegans*), and other North American turtles.

A better understanding of the order over all will only be made possible by the study of chelonians found in other parts of the world, such as Africa. As many species occurring in Third World areas represent an important potential source of protein and other nutrients for the native peoples, such research would not be merely of academic interest. It could lead, in the future, to the ranching of chelonians, perhaps in areas where other forms of livestock enterprise would not be feasible. The potential husbandry difficulties likely to be encountered would probably be less than those presently faced by marine-turtle ranching enterprises. In this way also, wild stocks would be maintained, and could even be supplemented from the breeding farms.

Chapter 3
Reproduction

In spite of their potentially long lifespan, chelonians may start breeding from about three years of age onwards, depending upon the species concerned. Captive-bred turtles often tend to breed at an earlier age than their wild counterparts, as they usually grow at a quicker rate. Sexual maturity in chelonians is more a reflection of size rather than age, although exceptions are known, as in the stinkpot turtle (*Sternotherus odoratus*), which appears to mature at about three years old, irrespective of size. There is no clearly definable pattern relating to size. The green turtle (*Chelonia mydas*) may breed when only four years old, and yet the smaller gopher tortoises (*Gopherus* spp) can wait as long as two decades before breeding for the first time.

Variations also exist in the growth rate, and hence the age of maturity, between different sexes of the same species. It is more common for males to mature earlier than females, and at a smaller size, as in the painted turtles (*Chrysemys picta*) and the diamondback terrapin (*Malaclemys terrapin*). This presumably increases the likelihood of successful matings.

There are exceptions to this generalisation, however, and differences even between members of the same genus have been noted. Female white-lipped mud turtles (*Kinosternon leucostomum*) are capable of breeding at a smaller size than their male counterparts, whereas there is no apparent difference in size in the case of the yellow mud turtle (*K. flavescens*). The underlying reason for these variations is unclear. It is tempting to suppose that females may have a shorter lifespan and therefore begin reproducing at an earlier stage. Certainly, they may be more vulnerable to predators, when they emerge to lay their eggs.

Sexual distinctions

There are various external anatomical means of distinguishing between the sexes in chelonians. Size, as mentioned previously, can be a useful indicator in this regard. In some species, such as Barbour's map turtle (*Graptemys barbouri*), the female is significantly larger than her mate, with a carapace length of 25 cm (10 in) or more. In contrast, males rarely grow beyond 11.25 cm (4½ in), and, interestingly, congregate along the sides of the rivers where they occur, whereas females inhabit deeper water. A similar situation is observed in the case of the Alabama map turtle (*G. pulchra*), with females taking much longer to mature than males. They only start breeding at about 14 years old, yet males are fertile when four years old.

The situation is reversed, but not to such an extreme degree, in the case of the gopher tortoises, *G. agassizii* and *G. berlandieri*. In only a few species, like the mud turtle (*Kinosternon hirtipes*), is there clear evidence that the size of the adults varies through their range. In certain populations, males are invariably bigger than females, and vice versa. A detailed study of populations of the stinkpot turtle (*Sternotherus odoratus*) revealed that males tended to be larger in northern areas, which had a mean annual temperature of between 7 and 13°C (44-55°F) approximately. In a more southerly and warmer locality, with a temperature in the range 21-23°C (70-73°F), females were bigger. No clear distinctions could be detected within the intervening populations. There is, again, no conclusive explanation for this trend, althouth the availability of food has been suggested as a factor.

Female turtles must reach a given size if they are to lay, because of the physical demands of egg production. The musk turtles, as a group, lay relatively small eggs in any event, and in small clutches. It therefore seems likely that a restriction on the availability of food in an area would be less crucial to the male, as maturation at a smaller size would be possible, compared with the case of the female.

In species where one member of a pair remains relatively small, adults may show clear distinctions in their pattern of markings. Those of smaller size tend to retain the more colourful appearance of immatures, whereas the larger turtles develop a relatively dull shell patterning.

The shape of the tail is another significant sexual characteristic, with males having a longer tail, which tends to be broader at its base to accommodate the penis. The cloacal opening is also situated further away from the body in the case of male turtles, when compared with their female counterparts. It is also not unusual for the plastron to be slightly concave in males, which presumably helps them to balance on the female's carapace when they are mating. In some tortoises, notably the gopher species (*Gopherus*), the gular prong at the front of the plastron is enlarged in males. This is used during mating, and also to deter rivals from pursuing a female, by battering them.

Another unusual feature of gopher tortoises is the presence of sexual glands on both sides of the lower surface of the jaw. These are clearly evident, and swell during the breeding period. They produce a secretion which acts as a scent marking. Males will rub their heads on objects within their range, and on females, transferring their scent. Female gopher tortoises may possess a specialised scale on each fore limb, which enables them to wipe secretions from their glands, and this appears to trigger an immediate response from the male. Having displayed by means of head bobbing, the male then switches to an attempt to bite the female, as a prelude to mating, when she responds in this way.

Other species of chelonian also possess similar glands, but they are relatively inconspicuous. Again, they are better developed in males than females, and have been identified in members of the families Emydidae and Platysternidae. It is thought that they function in a similar way to those present in gopher tortoises.

Plate 38 A young loggerhead musk turtle (*Sternotherus minor*) at two weeks of age. It is likely to be another three or four years before it will be able to breed for the first time. Maturity in chelonians tends to be correlated more closely to size than age.

Seasonal colour variations

An unusual colour change is associated with breeding male Asian river turtles (*Callagur borneoensis*), a species which is also sexually dimorphic. They tend to be greyish-brown in colour for much of the year, with females and juveniles being more brownish and clearly distinguishable. At the onset of the breeding period, however, these large emydid turtles develop a carapace which is cream in colour. Their heads are also transformed, becoming white with a prominent bright red stripe down the centre, edged with black. It appears that this area is highly vascularised at this stage, as touching the stripe causes the colour to fade temporarily. It rapidly returns, when the pressure is lifted, effectively confirming that it results from blood flow.

This alteration in appearance is not unique, being known to occur in the related tuntong turtle (*Batagur baska*). Indeed, it has been suggested that the distinctive change in colorations of male Asian river turtles might have evolved so that females could distinguish between these two species, which are found in the same area. The tuntong turtle becomes black over all, rather than white, at the onset of the breeding period.

The effect of testosterone injections is to mimic the changes seen naturally in male Asian river turtles. This confirms that the alteration in colour stems, at least in part, from the hormonal surge associated with breeding behaviour. The scutes of the carapace are shed at this time, and grow back much lighter in colour. The cells producing the pigment melanin disappear from the skin, the epidermal layer of which thickens considerably in breeding males. With this build-up in the outer skin layer, and the loss of melanin, which is then confined to the dermis beneath, dark coloration is effectively masked during this period.

It may be that in these turtles, which inhabit rivers rather than still stretches of water, differences in coloration serve as more potent indicators of sexual activity than pheromones produced by glands, which would be lost in the current. It is interesting that the batagur still possesses mental glands which are present on each side of the lower jaw, and responsible for the production of these sexually attractive chemical scents, however, so the importance of olfactory cues has apparently not been totally lost. Females have much smaller mental glands, which appear to be non-functional.

Other sexual characteristics

Physical attributes which may also serve to attract a mate are evident in *Chrysemys* turtles and related species. The front claws of males are noticeably elongated, to the point of appearing overgrown. These form an integral part of the display pattern in such turtles, being used to fan water towards the female, and even in stroking her head directly.

In contrast, there seems no obvious explanation for the difference in colour of the irides of Eastern box turtles (*Terrapene carolina*). As mentioned previously, males have organish-red irides, whereas those of females are essentially brownish. The ornate box turtle (*T. ornata*) differs slightly, in that females have yellowish irides. Some authors suggest the division between the sexes, on the basis of eye colour alone, is not entirely reliable and needs to be considered in conjunction with other features, such as the plastral and tail shapes.

The male chelonian

The copulatory organ is normally retained within the cloaca, and gives a swollen base to the tail of male chelonians. The elongated and flexible tail, with the cloacal opening situated at some distance along its length from the body, assists in the correct positioning of the penis during mating. Some species, such as the green turtle (*Chelonia mydas*) and members of the family Kinosternidae, have evolved auxiliary means of support, such as elongated claws, to help them to remain in position during mating. When blood flow to the penis increases as a result of sexual excitement, the organ is then extruded, in a downward and slightly cranial direction. Attempts have been made to group chelonians on the basis of their penile morphology, as this is a distinctive characteristic, but the method has not proved entirely satisfactory in the light of known classificatory relationships.

The actual production of sperm, known as spermatogenesis, tends to be seasonal. Not surprisingly, it begins in the spring and continues through to the end of the summer, reaching a peak at this stage. The process then declines, and hibernating chelonians store spermatozoa not in their testes, but in the epididymides. This is used during the early part of the following year, having remained viable throughout the winter.

The reproductive cycle is under hormonal control. Two different hormonal influences may be required, the initial activity being triggered by follicle stimulating hormones in the spring. Once the spermatocytes have formed in the paired testes, the interstitial cells here produce androgen, which enables the maturation process to be completed, and spermatozoa result. The activity of the interstitial cells is influenced by the level of luteinizing hormone in the circulation.

The female chelonian

Relatively little study has been carried out into the reproductive physiology of chelonians in general, and this also applies to the female's reproductive cycle. In most fresh-water species, it appears that they will normally nest each year, but some exceptions, such as the alligator snapping turtle (*Macroclemys temmincki*), have been reported. Females of this species are said to lay every second year. More prolonged cycles are known to exist in the case of sea turtles. In many cases, green turtles (*Chelonia mydas*) only return to nest every three years on average, although deviations on either side of this figure are not unknown. It may be for this reason that these turtles lay relatively large clutches when they do come ashore for breeding purposes.

Various distinctive stages occur in the build-up to egg-laying, certainly in temperate species which, again, have been more intensively studied. Follicles in the ovaries show initial signs of development, with the laying down of yolk, a process known as vitellogenesis. This typically begins towards the end of the summer, and may be completed before hibernation commences, depending on local environmental factors. Indeed, in turtles occurring in more southerly latitudes, the process is more likely to be evident after the chelonians have emerged from hibernation, rather than beforehand.

If the female is to lay more than one clutch of eggs, follicles in different stages of development will be visible within the ovary. As one set matures and is laid, so another comes closer to completing its period in the ovary. There is, however, no clear pattern of alternating ovulation from each ovary in turn. Once expelled from one ovary, the ova may actually transfer to the other oviduct, although the reason for this is unclear. It could possibly serve to balance the number of ova present within the tract.

The production of ova is not followed by immediate egg-laying. Studies suggest that it can take several weeks, possibly as long as two months in the case of the stinkpot turtle (*Sternotherus odoratus*), for the eggs to complete the final stages of their development.

There is thus no clear overlap between the male and female reproductive cycles. The development of ova, beginning in the later part of the summer, occurs just as the production of spermatozoa is in decline. There is a gap, often described as the latent period, between ovulatory cycles. In northern parts of its range, the painted turtle (*Chrysemys picta*) may have only a month between the development of sets of follicles, whereas this timespan is lengthened in the south, extending to as long as three months.

While some chelonians such as the common snapping turtle (*Chelydra serpentina*), show distinct cycles in this respect, others, including species from tropical areas, appear capable of nesting throughout the year. A significant factor, which influences successful egg-laying, is the ability of the females of at least some species to retain fertile spermatozoa within their bodies. They can produce viable eggs for as long as four years after their last mating. This unusual phenomenon has been observed in the common snapping turtle (*Chelydra serpentina*), and the common box turtle (*Terrapene carolina*), and may well apply to other species also.

As many chelonians lead fairly solitary lives, this means that females can take advantage of favourable breeding conditions, even in the absence of a male. It also assists in the overall spread of the species, as a female moved to a favourable habitat, perhaps because of flooding, for example, can establish a new population in this area on her own.

Temperature as a breeding stimulus

In individual chelonians, temperature appears to be the most important constraining factor on the reproductive cycle, especially in species occurring in temperate areas. In the painted turtle (*Chrysemys picta*), as in other species, the actual effects of temperature variations elicit different responses between the sexes and there is clear seasonal variation in their reproductive physiologies. In males, the beginning of spermatogenesis requires a body temperature in excess of 17°C (63°F), and at 28°C (82°F), full testicular activity would be restored in the spring within a period of seven weeks. Spermatogenesis begins earlier in more southerly populations, where the temperature is higher, and lasts over a longer period.

The situation is significantly different in female painted turtles, however, as the higher temperature which stimulates spermatogenesis actually inhibits ovarian activity. At a figure not exceeding 17°C (63°F), development of the ova, and then ovulation, proceed normally in the spring. Follicular growth does occur at lower temperatures, as would be anticipated during the autumn, but ovulation does not then take place until the spring. Appetite and food intake appear to exert no effect on reproductive activity, as both sexes feed more avidly at 28°C (82°F).

Field studies with this species, in Virginia, showed that vitellogenesis began in August and, apart from a break during hibernation, continued through to May. Egg-laying in the population began during the middle of the month and extended through to July. Some females laid twice during this period, and the second clutch of eggs tended to be slightly larger than the first.

The importance of the overwintering of spermatozoa in the epididymides of males is probably greater in more northerly populations. Breeding behaviour is usually seen soon after the turtles have emerged from hibernation, when the temperature would be too low to permit spermatogenesis to take place. As in other species, the larger females tend to produce bigger clutches, and their eggs are also larger.

Similar reproductive trends have been recorded in other North American species, such as the eastern spiny soft-shell turtle (*Trionyx s. spiniferus*). In males of this species, the testes underwent an eightfold growth as spermatogenesis began in April, and peaked during the following August. Regression then occurred, with this stage being completed by November. Within the females of this Tennesseean population, it tended to be the larger individuals which laid more than one clutch of eggs.

The influence of light exposure, termed photoperiod, on the reproductive behaviour of chelonians is less clear. It may have some influence in temperate species, although there is little variation in the case of separate slider populations (*Trachemys scripta*), occurring both in North America and in the tropics, where day length is more constant. This tends to suggest that its impact is minimal, at least in the case of this species. It seems that internal regulatory mechanisms are more significant, especially as most temperate species breed within the same period.

Pairing and hybridisation

The more mature chelonians within a population tend to be reproductively active for longer than smaller individuals. There appears to be no strong pair bond in the majority of cases, although male Florida gopher tortoises (*Gopherus polyphemus*) are known to visit specific females within their range for mating purposes, even if the female has actually moved during the intervening period. In this instance, there is an order of dominance, with the larger males driving off smaller rivals.

Rather than entering the burrow of the female, which could lead to an aggressive response, the male encourages his potential mate to emerge by means of head movements, and probably also through pheromones released from the mental glands. These glands are most developed in this genus, and enlarge during the breeding season. The glandular secretions which discharge directly on to the male's skin are wiped close to the female's burrow, and usually directly on her once she is above ground. Females show no particular preference for mates, accepting several in succession during the breeding period. As the spermatozoa may remain viable for long periods in the reproductive tract of females, it is tempting to suppose that a clutch could be fertilised by more than one male, although this appears not actually to have been proven as yet.

Scent is probably the most important trigger for courtship and mating, although, presumably, visual recognition of a potential mate is also significant in the first instance. The gopher tortoises (*Gopherus* spp) have all evolved slightly different scents and display movements of the head, presumably so that members of the same species could recognise each other without difficulty, thus avoiding accidental hybridisation. This would have been significant during the Pleistocene Period, when their areas of distribution overlapped, being wider than they are today.

Hybridisation does occasionally occur in chelonians as shown by the offspring from some eggs collected for the Cayman Turtle Farm Ltd. As the eggs appeared not to differ from those normally laid by green turtles (*Chelonia mydas*), it now seems likely that they were produced by a female of this species.

The young turtles which hatched soon proved highly aggressive, and differed obviously from green turtles in terms of their coloration. Other visual differences, such as the presence of two claws on each of the front flippers, rather than one, as in the green turtle, also suggested that they were hybrids. This view was supported by biochemical tests, and it was concluded that these turtles were the product of a mating between a hawksbill turtle (*Eretmochelys imbricata*) and a green turtle. It seems unlikely, in view of the size of the eggs, that they were laid by a hawksbill female, as her eggs would have been significantly smaller than those of a green turtle.

Out of the 37 recognisable hybrids, all appear to have been males. This may have been a reflection of the incubation temperature, or else there may be a lethal genetic factor precluding the viability of female offspring.

One of the interesting results of this discovery is that it clearly indicates a close relationship between these two species. Taxonomists have long argued as to whether the hawksbill is more appropriately included in the Chelonini sub-family, or grouped with members of the Carettini. The former relationship now appears more correct.

Hybridisation in the case of land tortoises is equally unusual, even where species are sympatric, or maintained together in a mixed group. Certainly, it does occur on occasions, and documented evidence reveals successful matings between marginated and Mediterranean spur-thighed tortoises (*Testudo marginata* and *T. graeca*), both in captivity and from the wild. Generally, however, males conspicuously avoid mating with females of the other species when both Hermann's (*T. hermanni*) and Mediterranean spur-thighed tortoises (*T. graeca*) are kept together.

Courtship and mating

When approaching a female tortoise closely, the male will sniff carefully around her cloacal region. It seems likely that where there is no clear sexual dimorphism, recognition of the individual's gender is achieved by olfactory means. Scent may be transferred from the cloaca to the hind legs of the individual, possibly providing a trail on the ground. Other factors, such as the maturity of the chelonian, may also be ascertained in this way. Sniffing around the head of a potential mate is also usually evident, but this tends to be of secondary importance, and may well be a direct prelude to the act of mating.

Copulation is often preceded by an aggressive display from males. They frequently attempt to bite at the limbs of their intended mates, sometimes causing physical injury. Shell butting, notably around the costal-supracaudal scute junction at the rear of the shell above the tail, is also evident. The male uses the gular prongs, or simply the intergular shields of his plastron for this purpose, withdrawing his head on each occasion. Old females may show a clear indentation on the shell in this area, where they have been repeatedly butted.

If the female does not respond by becoming quiescent, the male may continue to pursue her over a considerable distance and often at relatively high speed. Study of the radiated tortoise (*Geochelone radiata*) has revealed that mating attempts can be made over a wide thermal range of 16-35°C (61-95°F). The degree of cloud cover appears insignificant, but mating is less likely to occur in this species during or after rainfall. Encounters are most common towards the end of the afternoon. There is a social structure within a group housed together, with certain males proving more dominant, and thus mating more often than others, irrespective of their size.

On occasions, one or other member of the pair may fall over onto its back during courtship. Usually, there is a pause while they right themselves, although, certainly in the case of the Mediterranean spur-thighed tortoise (*Testudo graeca*), a male may continue battering a female until she regains her feet.

Once the female appears stationary, the male is likely to attempt to mount her. In the case of aquatic species, with their flattened shells, males may continue to snap at the female's neck from above. This obviously tends to immobilise the female, and could help to keep the male in position. The actual mating posture varies according to the species concerned. Balance, in the case of members of the Kinosternidae family, is assisted by the presence of supportive pads on the inner surface of the hind feet.

The box turtles of the genus *Terrapene* have a particularly difficult task when mating, as not only do they have a domed shell, but also the tail of the male is relatively short. As a result, he is forced to adopt an almost vertical stance, supporting himself by hooking his hind claws firmly in the space between the female's carapace and plastral hinge. She, in turn, reinforces his tenuous grip by providing additional support with her hind limbs.

68

The long claws of male *Chrysemys* turtles appear to be more significant in courtship than mating. Having swum backwards in front of the female, fanning water towards her face with gentle movements of his front legs, the male then follows his mate, eventually adopting the characteristic mating posture. The claws are then used to hold the female around the borders of her carapace.

The difference in size between partners of some species could be advantageous during mating. Small males may find it easier to retain their balance on top of a larger female's carapace. This might apply especially in the case of aquatic species, which invariably mate in water, as natural size differentials are more pronounced in these chelonians than in tortoises.

When they are mating, male tortoises often roar, as in the case of the giant Galapagos species (*Geochelone elephantopus*). The significance of these sounds is unclear. They are of short duration, lasting about 3/10ths of a second in the case of the radiated tortoise (*Geochelone radiata*). Measurement of the frequencies of these calls has revealed that they usually fall within the range of sounds audible to chelonians, ranging from 300 to 1200 Hz. It is likely that they may be a means of communicating with other chelonians in the area. The calls may be part of a series, as in the radiated tortoise, or an almost continual call-note, as uttered by the Mediterranean spur-thighed tortoise (*Testudo graeca*).

Once the male is in position for mating, the tail is used as a probe to establish contact with the female's cloacal opening, enabling intromission to take place. Having found the opening, the tip of the tail penetrates for a short distance, while the penis itself is everted. Then, by tracking down the caudal groove of the female, the penis is ultimately inserted into the cloaca, which has already been dilated by the tail. Once penetration has taken place, the tip of the tail is held under the plastron of the female, helping to anchor the male's organ in place.

Mating can be a protracted process, with the chelonians remaining joined for over an hour, particularly in aquatic species. Tortoises often mate for shorter periods, but may copulate repeatedly throughout the day. There is little actual movement evident once penetration has taken place, until the male dismounts. The chelonians then tend to go their separate ways.

If a female does not want to mate, she usually withdraws her hind feet and lowers her shell, making it virtually impossible for the probing tail of the male to reach her cloacal opening. She may also move from side to side, while remaining virtually stationary, in an attempt to dislodge the male. This movement can also prevent a male from climbing onto her back in the first instance. In many cases, however, the male is not deterred, and will eventually be accepted by the female after persistent attempts at mounting her. There is some evidence to suggest that the repeated shell butting may trigger a physiological response in the female, even stimulating the development of ova within her ovaries. Making attempts over a period of time, therefore, may bring the female into a receptive condition.

Plate 39   A pair of African spurred tortoises (*Geochelone sulcata*) mating. After an initial period of shell butting and snapping at the female's legs, the male will mount her. Repeated matings may take place during the course of a day.

The relative numbers of each sex within a population may exert an influence on reproductive strategy. A relatively large number of males could be anticipated in a situation where repeated mating attempts stimulated breeding behaviour in females. Conversely, as females of some species can reproduce without mating again on each occasion, a preponderance of females could be anticipated within any given population.

While this area of chelonian reproduction has not been well studied, it is perhaps worth noting that in the diamondback terrapin (*Malaclemys terrapin*), which is known to be able to breed for several years after a single mating, the sex ratio does appear to favour females. In a large sample of 1,433 individuals, females outnumbered males by nearly six to one.

The egg

All chelonians reproduce by means of eggs. After fertilisation has occurred, the ovum becomes transformed into the egg by the addition of various layers, and notably the shell, during its passage through the oviduct. Albumen is incorporated alongside the yolk containing the fertilised zygote, with the encasing shell membranes being included before the shell itself is added. Passage through the oviduct may take a fortnight, during which time the embryo begins its development.

The consistency of the shell is variable. It can be hard and brittle if the shell membranes have been infiltrated with calcium salts. Eggs with parchment shells are far less rigid in structure. They can swell with water early on in the incubation period, and are rubbery in texture. They are much less likely to break if dropped than the brittle-shelled

Plate 40   An X-ray showing a number of eggs within the body of a spurred tortoise (*Geochelone sulcata*). Knowledge about the reproductive behaviour and requirement of chelonians has advanced greatly during recent years.

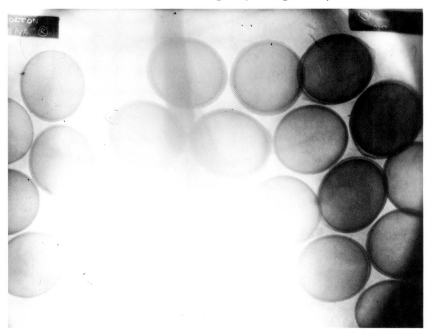

eggs. A third category of eggshell also exists, with characteristics which are intermediate between these two forms. They may initially appear hard, but actually swell quite considerably during the incubation period, like the parchment-shelled egg.

These differences can be explained by analysis of the relative proportions of minerals present in the shell. The thickness of deposition is increased in eggs with hard, rigid shells, compared with those which are protected by a parchment covering. The hard, yet expansible eggs have a shell of intermediate thickness.

Although some chelonians only produce eggs of one shell type, others are capable of varying the shell texture. In the common snapping turtle (*Chelydra serpentina*), for example, the southern Florida species, *C. s. osceola*, is characterised by laying eggs with hard yet expansible shells. The nominate race, *C. s. serpentina*, occurring in Minnesota, produces parchment-shelled eggs. Individual females may even differ in this regard, which tends to suggest that such changes could be the result of dietary differences influencing the availability of mineral salts. Alternatively, the distinctions may reflect the variable length of time that the eggs have spent in the oviduct. Those obtained from gravid females prior to laying usually have parchment-type shells, irrespective of how they may ultimately appear once they are laid.

The appearance of the shell surface is another variable characteristic, and may be smooth or nodular, irrespective of the shell type itself. Generally, however, brittle eggs tend to have smooth surfaces, whereas

Plate 41 A section through the egg in Plate 43. Note the abnormal shell thickness, and the yolk within. There is no sign of an embryo here. It is believed that chilling can cause the egg to become malformed in this way, because its passage through the reproductive tract is delayed, leading to excessive shell deposition.

those with parchment shells are superficially nodular. Pores are also evident in the eggs of many species, and allow loss of fluid from the interior during the incubation period, as has been noted in the case of the starred tortoise (*Geochelone elegans*). Gases and water are liable to move across the shells of both types of egg, although brittle eggs maintain their shape even if there is a net loss of fluid, whereas parchment-type eggs show signs of indentation.

It has been suggested that the increased flexibility of the parchment-shelled egg is utilised during the egg-laying process, enabling females to expel large eggs from their bodies. These could subsequently harden, to form brittle-shelled eggs of a bigger overall diameter. This theory is no longer accepted, however, as it has been shown that in order to lay eggs, the rigid shell structure of various species, such as the emydid *Rhinoclemmys* turtles, becomes softened around the cloaca area. As a result, females can lay their relatively big eggs without fear of becoming egg-bound. A similar phenomenon is seen in birds, where the pelvic bones of laying hens dilate to permit the passage of eggs.

The shape of the chelonian's egg tends to vary, and is clearly related to clutch size. Those species which produce rounded eggs, such as the marine turtles and the Arrau River turtle (*Podocnemis expansa*), often lay well in excess of ten eggs per clutch. In contrast, chelonians which have longer, more cylindrical-shaped eggs, have fewer per clutch. Clearly, the elongated egg will occupy more space within the oviduct, whereas spherical eggs can be more numerous. Again, variations within a species are detectable, as shown by the spineless soft-shell (*Trionyx muticus*).

In this instance, the northern populations have more spherical eggs than those occurring further south, and lay, on average, perhaps 20 in a clutch. In southern parts of their range, these soft-shells may only lay five or six eggs at a time. Presumably, a potentially greater number of offspring are required in northern waters in order to maintain the population's numbers.

A few species lay eggs which are not evenly elongated, but are narrower at one end, like a bird's egg. These include the South American twist-neck turtle (*Platemys platycephala*) and the big-headed turtle (*Platysternon megacephalum*). Considerable variation may also be seen in the eggs of tortoises, especially hingeback (*Kinixys*) species. They lay elongated eggs, which may differ quite considerably in shape.

The actual number of eggs in a clutch depends on the species concerned. The pancake tortoise (*Malacochersus tornieri*) lays just one egg, whereas, at the other extreme, marine turtles may produce over 200 eggs in a single clutch. The amazing total of 242 was counted from a hawksbill turtle (*Eretmochelys imbricata*) nesting on Cousin Island, part of the Seychelles group.

Clutch size is influenced to a certain extent by the carapace length of the female chelonian. It is clear that, generally, the larger females lay bigger clutches, and also have bigger eggs in some cases. In terms of individual size, chelonians occurring in arid areas of the world generally produce eggs which are slightly smaller than chelonians of equivalent

Plate 42   A clutch of eggs laid by a female Mediterranean spur-thighed tortoise. Note the small non-viable egg in the centre. These are not uncommon in the case of chelonians. The leatherback turtle (*Dermochelys coriacea*), in particular, often lays a significant number of malformed eggs in each clutch.

size in tropical areas with higher rainfall. Hatchlings from bigger eggs tend themselves to be larger, and thus have a better chance of survival.

The environment may also exert a considerable influence on the reproductive capacity of the chelonian. Whereas the desert tortoise (*Gopherus agassizii*) may produce up to 13 eggs in a clutch, its relative, the Texas tortoise (*G. berlandieri*) tends to lay only one or two eggs. The populations of this particular tortoise are quite isolated, for geographical reasons, and there appears to be little movement between established groups. This, in turn, means that their range is limited, and the food supply is equally restricted. Clearly, if the species regularly produced a

Plate 43   Another abnormal egg. In this case, the shell itself is unduly thickened, and forms a point at one end. Eggs of this type are not likely to be viable. Under normal circumstances, chelonian eggs should be moved carefully, and not turned at all throughout the incubation period.

large number of offspring, this would soon threaten its survival, by reducing the available grazing, as populatory migrations do not normally occur. It is therefore possible that this particular species has evolved its low reproductive ability to favour its survival in this area.

Imprinting and socialisation studies

The female alone is responsible for selecting the nesting site. In the case of marine turtles, she invariably returns to the beach where she herself hatched, often decades before. Unfortunately, this renders her highly vulnerable, especially to human predation. While turtles reared in captivity can be mature by the age of eight years old, it appears that it may be much longer, possibly 40 years in a few cases, before wild turtles commence breeding. It has long been a source of mystery as to how these giants, having roamed the world's oceans for decades, maintain such a strong homing instinct.

The traditional explanation is that at a crucial early stage in their development, hatching turtles learn to recognise their hatching beach before they enter the sea, and this memory is indelibly etched into their consciousness, to be recalled decades later. A more recent explanation is based on a sociability theory, involving communication between individual turtles. This suggests that young turtles, ready to breed for the first time, meet and follow adults to the nesting sites. In turn, they themselves learn how to navigate to these beaches, and thus are able to transfer their knowledge, later, to other turtles. Known as the social facilitation model, this theory draws support from the fact that turtles would thus need only a relatively short memory, rather than relying on information imprinted perhaps four decades previously.

Another positive aspect of the social facilitation explanation, which could assist the population over all, is that new nesting sites could be developed quite easily. Adults may arrive at new localities, either by chance or because stormy weather prevented them from reaching their original preferred locality. If conditions were then favourable, they could return in following years, bringing young turtles with them.

It is likely that a much clearer indication of the relative merits of these two explanations will emerge within the next few years, as a result of an attempt to translocate a population of the severely endangered species, Kemp's ridley turtle (*Lepidochelys kempi*). These turtles, whose distribution is centred on the Gulf of Mexico, breed naturally at Rancho Nuevo, Tamaulipas, Mexico, where, for over two decades, their nesting sites have been guarded.

During 1978, it was decided to attempt to set up an artificial new satellite breeding colony in the United States. The location chosen was Padre Island, Texas. The scheme began in earnest in 1979, when 1,855 eggs, about 2 per cent of the total laid in Mexico, were used to initiate the American project. The resulting 1,461 turtles were released during the following year. This figure is actually in excess of the likely survival rate of all the remaining eggs left in Mexico.

Part of the problem in investigating the breeding habits of turtles is the difficulty in marking small hatchlings which will increase ten thousandfold in weight by adulthood. It has been possible, using radio-tracking, to monitor the progress of the young turtles in the Padre Island experiment for a period, and initial results tend to indicate that they have established themselves well. Time will tell whether, in the absence of experienced adults, they are able to navigate back to the beaches here.

Sociability may be particularly important in this species, as egg-laying is preceded by mass beaching of the gravid females. Up to 40,000 are estimated to have been present on one occasion on a stretch of beach just 1.6 km (1 mile) long. The success of the Padre Island release may not be evident for several years yet, as it is unclear as to when this species becomes mature. Previous schemes of this type, which began in 1954, involving hatchling green turtles (*Chelonia mydas*), have proved largely inconclusive.

A number of fresh-water chelonians also undertake seasonal move-

Plate 44 A nesting site for fresh-water turtles in Queensland, Australia. Aquatic species generally choose to lay their eggs on relatively high ground, so that the nesting site will not be swamped if the water level rises.

ments during the breeding period. The batagur (*Batagur baska*) is known to migrate regularly, and similar excursions have been reported in other species, including the slider (*Trachemys scripta*) and painted turtle (*Chrysemys picta*). The common snapping turtle (*Chelydra serpentina*) may undertake a journey of 16 km (10 miles) at this stage, in order to reach the nesting site, travelling overland for at least part of this distance. The means by which the turtles orientate themselves and are able to return to their home range is poorly understood. It may be that the mechanism of imprinting, as suggested for marine species, could also apply to their fresh-water counterparts.

Plate 45   A female Mediterranean spur-thighed tortoise (*Testudo graeca*)
preparing a nesting site. The hind limbs are used to dig the hole in a laborious
fashion. At this stage, the tortoise tends to lose much of its natural shyness.

Plate 47   The female carefully covers her eggs afterwards, so that it is
impossible to locate the nest easily. She then takes no further interest in them,
except in the case of the Burmese brown tortoise (*Geochelone emys*), which stays
close to the nesting site for several days, attempting to drive off any creatures
which become curious about the nesting mound.

Plate 46 The completed nesting chamber, with eggs visible inside. The actual laying process is speedily accomplished, the eggs being voided with mucus, which serves to protect them from breaking as they are deposited in the nesting hollow.

Plate 48　The nesting chamber after it has been excavated to allow the eggs to be removed and incubated artificially. It is now clear that the incubation temperature is critical in determining the gender of the offspring in many species, although no clear pattern exists.

The nest

The female constructs the nesting hollow on her own, tending to use her hind feet for this purpose. Only the Burmese brown tortoise (*Geochelone emys*) is believed to use its fore feet for this task, having selected a suitable site. This species is also unusual in that it shows a primitive degree of parental concern. After laying her eggs, the female piles up earth over them, and stays in the vicinity for several days, apparently deterring potential predators by her presence. Her interest soon wanes, however, and she leaves the eggs to their fate well before the end of the incubation period.

Nest digging is a laborious process, and renders the chelonian clearly exposed to predators at this time. The site chosen, therefore, is often relatively concealed, certainly in the case of aquatic species, which can be particularly vulnerable out of water. Marine turtles tend to nest during a high tide. This will carry them further onto the shore, and they are thus likely to be able to spend the minimum of time on nest-construction, also choosing a site which should be out of reach of the waves. Turtles tend to avoid an area of vegetation, as roots can prove a barrier to nest-building, or sloping land, where their nests could be washed away in a heavy storm.

Chelonians will lay in virtually any type of soil, although they prefer sandy areas, which are probably easier to work than heavy clay soils. Most marine turtles make a point of sniffing the sand on the beach before commencing nesting operations in earnest. This may be an olfactory recognition response, tied in with their homing instinct. Alternatively, they may simply be searching for the most favourable locality, scenting as to whether other turtles have beached here before them, and may already have laid. They will often move ponderously for a considerable distance before actually deciding upon the nesting site. This affords additional protection against high tides, which could otherwise flood the nest.

Marine turtles generally prefer a locality which is in direct sunlight. Whether this may help to orientate the young turtles when they emerge from the nesting site is unclear. Some fresh-water species also prefer a similarly bright location, including the map turtles (*Graptemys geographica* and *G. pseudogeographica*). They may not stray far from water, as shown by the case of the smooth soft-shell (*Trionyx muticus*), which usually lays within 30 m (100 ft) of its aquatic habitat.

Prior to the construction of the nesting chamber where the eggs will be laid, some chelonians, notably the sea turtles, excavate a shallow hollow in which they can lie. Described as the body pit, this is normally excavated using the front limbs only, although, apparently, the ornate box turtle (*Terrapene ornata*) uses its hind limbs only for this task.

The hind limbs then work in synchrony to prepare the nesting chamber, except in the case of the radiated tortoise (*Geochelone radiata*). This species does not alternate the use of its limbs, but digs with one until it becomes tired, and then changes over to the other. The earth is scooped up around the sides of the hole, with the chamber beneath ground level being larger than the opening on top. This is a useful way of ensuring that the hole is dug with minimum effort, yet maximum efficiency. If the tortoise encounters an obstruction during the excavation, she will often leave the site and begin again elsewhere. Indeed, several holes may be started before egg-laying actually occurs.

A number of species of both land and aquatic chelonian will urinate into the nest hole during the excavation process. Various reasons have been proposed to explain this behaviour. It serves to soften the ground initially, and may make digging easier, especially if the soil is dry and well compacted. However, some Australian fresh-water turtles prefer to abandon a nesting attempt under these circumstances. The urine could also serve to conceal any scent of the eggs from predators, as well as providing moisture in the nest, increasing the humidity here. Certainly, a relatively high humidity is a prerequisite for hatching, even in the case of species inhabiting arid areas. In addition, by softening and then breaking down the soil into small particles, the chelonian is better able to conceal its nest after egg-laying.

In the Galapagos Islands, the tortoises actually move to specific areas where egg-laying is possible. Urination is probably essential in this species just to produce suitable ground conditions for the construction of the nesting chamber. Under the heat of the sun, the top of the nesting site then sets quite hard, and could help to prevent predators reaching the eggs. The only clear example of possible nest concealment is seen in the Peninsula slider (*Pseudemys floridana peninsularis*). Here, individual eggs are laid at a short distance away from the main nesting site.

Egg-laying

Having actually commenced laying, chelonians lose their natural caution, and continue almost totally oblivious of their surroundings. In cases where there is normally no predation, as in the case of the Ascension Island population of the green turtle (*Chelonia mydas*), the turtles show this behaviour right from emergence from the ocean. Other populations of the same species remain more nervous until the egg-laying process actually begins.

Eggs are laid in quite rapid succession, and are deliberately channelled into the breeding chamber by careful positioning of the hind legs in many species. The mucoid fluid voided along with the eggs helps to prevent those with hard, brittle shells from being broken as they are laid on top of each other. The hind legs are also used to close over the entrance to the nesting chamber, so that the site is fully concealed when the chelonian leaves it. The time of laying can also help to disguise the eggs, with marine turtles coming ashore at night to lay, and returning to the sea by the following dawn.

The incubation period

The length of time taken for the eggs to hatch is variable, depending partly on the species concerned and the environmental temperature. More northerly populations of the same species tend to show shorter incubation periods, typically not exceeding 110 days. Chelonians which lay brittle eggs invariably have a longer incubation period, possibly with the extra rigidity of the shell proving advantageous in this regard.

The environment where the eggs are laid also appears to exert an influence on the length of time they take to hatch. Those which are vulnerable to the elements, as in the case of marine turtles, develop quite rapidly. This observation can also be applied to fresh-water chelonians, as exemplified by the Arrau River turtle (*Podocnemis expansa*). This large species can only breed during the dry season, when the water level in the rivers falls sufficiently to expose the sandbanks where nesting takes place. The length of time taken for the reproductive cycle to be completed, before the sandbanks are submerged again, is possibly less than eight weeks.

In order to avoid being drowned in their nests, the young turtles have to develop rapidly, emerging within about six weeks, before the water level changes. Where the environmental pressure is reduced, the incubation period may be extended. The eggs of the Galapagos giant tortoise (*Geochelone elephantopus*), for example, take 30 weeks to hatch under normal circumstances.

In temperate areas, the incubation period may be artificially prolonged because of climatic factors. Hatchlings can remain buried in the nest site over the winter until the following spring. In more southerly temperate localities, the development of the eggs themselves may slow down during the winter period, delaying the actual hatching time.

The significance of incubation temperature

In mammals, as well as birds, the sex of the individual is determined by means of sex chromosomes. However, examination of the cell nucleus of chelonians has revealed that, in most cases, this particular pair of chromosomes appears not to be present. A notable exception has been observed in certain mud turtles (Kinosternidae), but this is not a standard feature of the family over all.

The incubation temperature of eggs is now known to be the vital factor in determining the sex of the hatchlings in many species, although no clear pattern is apparent. Indeed, in the members of the soft-shell genus *Trionyx*, development proceeds irrespective of temperature modification. In contrast, male offspring tend to predominate in the hatchlings of painted turtles (*Chrysemys picta*) if the eggs are kept at 28°C (82°F), whereas above 30°C (86°F) female offspring will be produced. In the intervening temperature range, hatchlings of either sex can be anticipated.

The situation varies again in the common snapping turtle (*Chelydra serpentina*), with males resulting if the eggs are maintained within the temperature range of 22-28°C (72-82°F). Outside these figures, female offspring can be anticipated.

A similar effect has been noted in land tortoises, including the Mediterranean spur-thighed (*Testudo graeca*). In this instance, female offspring result at a higher temperature, around 31-32°C (87.8-89.6°F), while below 30°C (86°F) male hatchlings are likely to be produced. Clearly a pattern of this type is of vital consideration in a captive-breeding project for endangered chelonians, when the eggs are being incubated artificially. By manipulating the environmental temperature, it should be possible, once the particular species' pattern is determined, to stimulate the production of females, and thus, ultimately, add considerably to the reproductive potential of the group.

The actual temperature variations are surprisingly small, however, and individuals which produce two clutches of eggs during the course of a year could obviously yield predominantly different sexes in each case, because of slight climatic alterations. It has been suggested, although there is no real evidence to support the theory, that female chelonians actually lay their eggs according to the needs of the population in the area concerned.

Temperature sex determination as a mechanism is suited to the needs of chelonians with their potentially long reproductive capacity. Over this period, the effects of slight variations in temperature during the breeding phase are likely to average out, so that there is no serious imbalance in the established sex ratio of the overall population.

Chelonians would be vulnerable to wide temperature variations, however, as a result of major climatic upheavals. This could explain the extinction of some species in the past, but it is likely that some regulatory mechanism is involved, as these reptiles, as a group, have survived for so long. The possible interrelationship between storage of spermatozoa and temperature sex determination has not apparently been investigated. Yet in a population with a relatively low density of males, as a result of the effects of temperature sex determination, the overall status of the species would not be threatened, as females could remain fertile.

It appears to be during the middle third of the incubation period that the eggs are most affected by temperature sex determination, but an influence can be exerted over a longer period. This may be a reflection of the depth of the nesting chamber. Sea turtles, for example, excavate a relatively deep hollow, and once the eggs are within this, they will experience little variation in temperature. Conversely, the superficial nest of a temperate fresh-water chelonian is more likely to be affected by wider temperature differentials through the incubation period.

Studies of the nests of marine turtles have confirmed that their offspring tend to be of one sex, as would be expected. But such is the density of egg-laying on certain beaches that invariably some clutches will be deposited in a somewhat more shaded place than others, which would help to correct any imbalance in the overall sex ratio of the hatchlings.

It has been suggested that the young chelonians might also undergo a change in gender during their maturation process, but this appears not to be the case. Once the influence of temperature has become apparent, there is no alteration in the individual's gender, irrespective of further temperature changes in its environment.

Viability of the eggs

In the wild there can be wide variations in the temperatures to which the eggs are exposed. The lower and upper thresholds for development to proceed normally similarly differ, depending on the species concerned. A study of nests of the Arrau River turtle (*Podocnemis expansa*) has revealed that, at a depth of 90 cm (3 ft), temperature variation is only 1°C (1.8°F), whereas superficial nests, close to the surface, can be subjected to fluctuations of as much as 23°C (41°F), up to 48°C (118°F). Eggs of the common snapping turtle (*Chelydra serpentina*), with a northerly distribution, will continue developing at a temperature of only 20°C (68°F), although this results in the death of the embryo prior to hatching. If the eggs are moved to a warmer temperature, however, they can still hatch normally. At the upper limit, a figure of 34°C (93°F) proves fatal for the embryos of this species.

Other factors, apart from temperature, will exert a direct influence on the viability of the eggs. Humidity is especially important in this regard, and levels of around 80 per cent relative humidity are required for eggs in incubator surroundings. The female's added fluid in the nest, by means of urination, may raise the humidity here. Yet heavy rainfall may cause flooding, which interferes with gaseous exchange, killing the embryos. Nestings of the green turtle (*Chelonia mydas*) on the coast of Borneo, for example, show a greatly reduced hatchability during the monsoon season. The turtle's preference for laying in sand rather than clay-based soils could help to minimise the effects of a tropical down-pour, as, clearly, the run-off of water will be quicker under these conditions, rather than creating puddles of standing water.

There are differences in the water permeability of the different shell types. Those with rigid shells can be incubated successfully on a bed of peat, for example, without desiccating, whereas water loss tends to be more pronounced in parchment-shelled eggs, which are best kept buried throughout the incubation period. It is generally accepted that chelonian eggs ought not to be turned, and, indeed, this procedure can have an adverse effect on hatchability, especially during the early stage of the incubation period.

While they are buried in the ground, the eggs are likely to be attacked by various micro-organisms, especially in view of the fairly lengthy incubation period, which may extend over the whole of the winter under certain circumstances. Little research has been carried out into how the egg can protect itself from this threat, but there is evidence to show that the albumen fraction contains antibiotics, which are effective against some bacteria. It may be that these tend to be specific for the type of micro-organism likely to be found in the species' natural range.

Studies in this field have concentrated on Horsfield's tortoise (*Testudo (Agrionemys) horsfieldi*), and have shown that antibiotic activity associated with the albumen fraction remains, irrespective of whether or not the egg is fertile. Various bacteria and other micro-organisms can penetrate the defences of the egg, however, and could presumably then infect the embryo. This aspect of immunity would need to be considered in trans-location work, as potentially low hatchability could otherwise result. Apart from the protection present in the albumen, however, the embryo itself may be able to mount some immune response, certainly during the later part of its development.

Hatching

Prior to actually emerging from the egg, the young chelonian breaks down the shell membranes, using the egg tooth, or more accurately the caruncle, visible as a small projection on the top of its nose. This structure soon regresses, once it has served its purpose in freeing the chelonian from the shell. After the initial tear, enabling air to enter through the crack, the hatchling will be able to force its way out of the shell. The length of time taken to break free can vary, and during this period the turtle's own shell begins to straighten out. It should escape from its shell within a day of the initial tear being apparent.

Traces of the yolk sac, which served to nourish the young chelonian through the incubation period, may still be apparent after hatching, being attached to the middle of the plastron. The food reserves here will continue to sustain the hatchling over the next few days, although during this period it will also begin to show an interest in solid food. The remnants of the yolk sac tend to vary somewhat, depending on the family concerned. In the mud turtles (Kinosternidae) little trace is evident, but in many other families, the remains are clearly visible. The yolk is drawn back into the body by the straightening of the two main shell components. The yolk is not actually responsible for the major

Plate 49   Throughout the incubation period, the yolk sac nourishes the developing chelonian embryo. Remnants which remain on hatching are rapidly utilised in the early days of life, so that the young chelonian does not immediately have to forage for food.

supply of calcium to the young chelonian. This is obtained directly from the egg shell, its inner surface being degraded for this purpose. Thinning of the shell through the incubation period could also assist in speeding the hatching process.

Under normal circumstances, the hatchability of chelonian eggs tends to be high. In the case of marine turtles, over 90 per cent of the eggs laid in the absence of predators may yield hatchlings. These then tunnel to the surface together and set out to reach the ocean. A significant proportion will not even get this far, however, being trapped by gulls and other predators, even crabs. But without the mass eruption of the young turtles onto the breeding beaches, the casualty toll could be much higher. A number are bound to escape the hazards, whereas small groups would be much more vulnerable.

The survival rate is influenced from the start by the size of the hatchlings. This strategy is exploited by the flat-backed turtle (*Chelonia depressa*), which produces relatively few eggs compared with the green turtle (*C. mydas*). A study of the nests of the flat-backed revealed an average clutch size of just 50, with the individual eggs being much bigger than those of related species. As a result, hatchling flat-backs are themselves significantly larger, and can escape the clutches of the two ghost crabs, which inhabit their nesting beaches, by virtue of their size. They are also less likely to fall prey to silver gulls (*Larus novaehollandiae*), which relentlessly pursue the smaller green turtles. When these species are fully grown, however, the flat-back is the smaller of the two.

The potential number of hatchlings which can be produced during the breeding period is enormous, as a number of clutches are usually laid in succession, possibly at intervals of only a fortnight. Loggerhead turtles (*Caretta caretta*) have been known to lay as many as six clutches through a season, averaging over 100 eggs in each.

Oceanic wanderings

Those hatchlings which do reach the sea also face many perils here, especially while they are small. Until recently, their actual whereabouts in these early days remained something of a mystery, known as the 'lost year', as they disappeared from sight. At first, their yolk sacs would sustain them, but it is clear from a study of loggerheads hatched on the South Georgia coastline of the United States that this food reserve is rapidly depleted. The turtles would be unable to reach the Gulf Stream current without feeding during the intervening period.

The earliest clue to the whereabouts of young turtles after leaving their nesting beaches emerged during 1968. A young loggerhead, which had recently hatched, was found in a raft of sargassum. Other similar discoveries were subsequently made, and the link between newly hatched turtles and these accumulations of seaweed was effectively confirmed by tracking hatchlings from their nesting beaches.

It now seems clear that the young chelonians swim rapidly out to sea, pausing only when they encounter a mat of sargassum weed. They then

Plate 50   A turtle nesting beach in the Seychelles. When they hatch, the young turtles unerringly head for the sea, rather than inland. It is possible that they respond to the sound of the waves on the shore, using this as a strong navigational cue.

Plate 51   The growth rate of young chelonians can vary quite widely. These two captive-bred spurred tortoises were hatched at the same time, and have been reared together under identical conditions. Similar discrepancies doubtless arise in the wild, where the food supply is likely to be variable, depending upon the area concerned.

remain here, feeding in the vicinity, and drifting in the ocean currents. Such occurrences have been noted in various parts of the world. Off the eastern seaboard of South Africa, however, both leatherback (*Dermochelys coriacea*) and loggerhead hatchlings have been observed floating in the Agulhas Current, moving southwards, although there is no sargassum here.

Elsewhere, further confirmation of the close links between sargassum mats and young turtles has been obtained following severe storms, which have deposited the weed, along with young turtles, on beaches. The evidence that the hatchlings are feeding in the weed is clear from study of their stomach contents. Apart from pieces of sargassum itself, invertebrates, such as the snail *Litiopa melanostoma*, known only in association with this weed, have been discovered here.

There are various routes that the hatchlings may take, depending on the direction of the currents, and it could be that, by tracking the currents on which they drifted, mature turtles might later be able to find their way back to the area where they were hatched. This explanation links both the imprinting and socialisation theories, as, clearly, a number of turtles could be tracking back along the same route almost together.

The number of hatchlings which actually survive to attain maturity is, however, very low. Estimates suggest that the likely survival rate is probably less than o.1 per cent, so that barely one out of every thousand hatchlings will return. This is obviously a major handicap to any study of a population, as vast numbers need to be marked and this can prove a costly enterprise. In addition, tags are likely to be lost during the intervening period, and not all hunters will return the tags when they catch a turtle. Human persecution is, in fact, the major threat to adult sea turtles, although they are also vulnerable to sharks and turtle remains have been found in killer whales, though the actual extent of this predation is uncertain.

Foetal malformations

The appearance of physical malformations in chelonian hatchlings is not uncommon. These can vary from mild abnormalities in shell structure, such as the pattern of the scutes, to double-headed monsters. Although this latter abnormality may sound especially gross, such turtles can live quite well, with both heads feeding. The most common form of this so-called 'conjoined twinning' is the situation where the two heads occur side by side, with the remainder of the turtle looking reasonably normal. The degree of fusion is highly variable. In some cases, the vertebral column itself may be divided, with duplication of the internal organs as well.

More unusual are chelonians joined at the rear ends of the shell, so that the heads are far apart and point in opposite directions. There can also be a plastral connection, which causes one of the heads to be in a permanently inverted position. The number of legs may also be increased, depending where fusion has occurred. In the wild, such creatures are most unlikely to survive for long, although they have been kept alive quite successfully in captivity. One false map turtle (*Graptemys pseudogeographica*) with two heads lived for about 18 months in the Staten Island Zoo in the United States. Each head was capable of feeding independently, and they would occasionally fight over a piece of food.

In these cases, surgical separation is clearly not feasible, and in spite of its monstrous appearance, the turtle can eat quite normally. Other congenital defects, such as cyclopia, where just one eye is present, often located in an abnormal position, and even herniation of the brain onto the outer surface of the skin on the top of the head, can be encountered occasionally.

Reasearch into these congenital defects has suggested that variations in temperature outside the usual range can prove the teratogenic trigger. The developing embryo appears most vulnerable at the stage when the organs are beginning to form. Dehydration may also have a role to play, at a slightly later stage of the development process. Although most accounts refer to fresh-water chelonians, the phenomenon of two heads, termed dicephalism, has also been reported on a couple of occasions in the angulate tortoise (*Chersina angulata*). Marine species could also be affected in a similar way, but the overall incidence of reptile dicephalism is much higher in snakes than in chelonians.

Chapter 4
The Evolution and Distribution of Chelonians

The early evolutionary history of chelonians is rather obscure, because of a lack of fossilised remains. However, it is known that these distinctive reptiles were already established by the start of the geological period known as the Triassic, at least 185 million years ago. It seems certain that they developed from the cotylosaurs, a primitive group known as the 'stem reptiles', because they were the forerunners of all contemporary reptiles. The origins of the cotylosaurs can, in turn, be traced back to the Carboniferous Period, about 100 million years before the Triassic. As far as the development of the chelonians is concerned, the intervening gap remains something of a mystery.

Cotylosaurs are believed to have been marsh-dwelling creatures. They had short, stocky limbs and a solid, or anapsid, roof to their skulls, with teeth present in their jaws. Chelonians resemble cotylosaurs in the lack of temporal openings, called fossae, in their skulls, and are classified in the sub-class Anapsida, alongside their extinct ancestors. Evolution has caused their teeth to be lost, and replaced instead by sharp, cutting jaws. Their body shape has become modified, with the rib cage being expanded and flattened and then encased in the characteristic shell.

The origins of chelonians

The traditional view of chelonian evolution was that a small fossilised creature, dating from the mid-Permian era, approximately 250 million years old, and living in present-day South Africa, provided the bridge back to the cotylosaurs. Named *Eunotosaurus africanus*, its remains suggested that it stood only about 10 cm (4 in) high and had broad ribs which served to increase the width of its body, like those of a modern chelonian. Yet the actual arrangement of the ribs, relative to the pectoral and pelvic girdles supporting the limbs, differs significantly from the arrangement seen in chelonians today. *Eunotosaurus* also appears to have lacked the protection provided by the shells of most chelonians.

Unfortunately, there is no complete fossil of *Eunotosaurus* available, and the appearance of a number of features, such as the top of the skull and its feet, is unknown. It has not even proved possible to establish that it had an anapsid skull, or an otic notch, other features associated with chelonians. It is now generally accepted, however, that *Eunotosaurus* did not feature directly in the ancestry of chelonians, but, instead, probably represented a parallel pathway in the evolutionary process, which came to a halt.

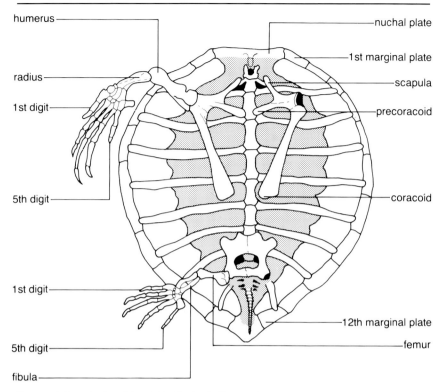

Fig. 5   The relationship of the limb girdles to the remainder of the skeleton is shown in a marine turtle.

More recent attention has been focused on a separate group of cotylosaurs, known as diadectomorphs. Various forms have been discovered, and although there is some doubt about their interrelationships, several significant features, shared with chelonians, have emerged from a study of these cotylosaurs. Their remains actually date from the Carboniferous Period through to the Triassic, when the first discernible chelonians emerged.

Diadectomorphs had no temporal openings on their skulls, and the otic notch, formed by modification of the quadrate bone, is here clearly discernible. The actual division between the early chelonians and this branch of the cotylosaurs must have taken place by the beginning of the Permian Period, however, as in later diadectomorphs the palate has fused with the upper part of the skull. This characteristic is not associated with chelonians, and so the group must have separated from its cotylosaur ancestors about 280 million years ago.

The armadillo theory

In the absence of convincing fossil evidence, there still remains the

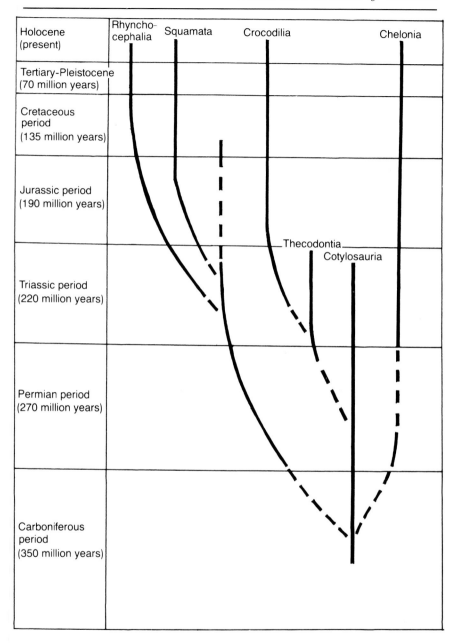

Fig. 6 The evolutionary pathway of chelonians and other contemporary reptiles. Broken lines indicate missing links in the evolutionary process.

possibility that the true ancestors of the chelonians have yet to be discovered. One theory based on this concept relies on an intermediate form, named the saurotestudinate, to explain the evolution of the chelonian's shell. It is generally agreed that the predecessors of today's chelonians originated in swampland. They may well have resembled broad-bodied lizards during the early stages of their development and this, in turn, gave rise to the description of saurotestudinate.

In support of the missing-link theory, a parallel has been drawn with armadillos, to explain the evolution of chelonians. These mammals' armour is in the form of bony plates, also known as scutes, which develop from the skin and are protected by a horny covering. This defensive casing does not extend over the whole of the body surface, however, and when directly threatened, some armadillos will curl up into a ball, protecting their soft, vulnerable underparts. Other species of armadillo simply drop down onto the ground, retracting their limbs under the protective body armour, just as tortoises, for example, do today.

As the primitive ancestors of the reptilian group ventured further onto land and away from their aquatic environment, they could have developed a similar protective skin covering, to compensate for their lack of speed. When threatened, these early chelonians would simply roll up, their skin casing becoming folded into scutes. The more advanced chelonian species, as in armadillos, would ultimately develop a means of withdrawing their limbs under their body casing, rather than curling into a ball.

This ingenious explanation of how chelonians acquired their shells actually loses some credibility, however, by drawing further on modern parallels in the absence of any fossil evidence. It has been suggested that the most primitive species of contemporary chelonian are those that remain essentially aquatic, and have never developed this hard protective armour. However, both the leather-backed turtle (*Dermochelys coriacea*) and the members of the family Trionychidae, commonly known as soft-shelled turtles, actually evolved from chelonians with rigid shells, and their shell structure has since become modified and softened.

Triassic chelonians

The earliest fossils that unmistakably resemble modern chelonians were found in Triassic deposits in present-day Germany. At this time, changes in the land masses were starting to occur, and these would have a significant impact on the distribution of chelonians as the group evolved. The two existing land masses, Gondwanaland and Laurasia, were still joined, and it is tempting to suppose that chelonians arose on the latter, northerly continent, as no remains dating back to the Triassic have been discovered outside the area of contemporary Europe.

The appearance of these early chelonians was basically similar to those seen today, although some distinctions can be drawn. They still had teeth present in both jaws, as well as on the palate itself. By this stage, the modified shape of the pectoral girdle is clearly evident, although the individual bones remain apparent, and signs of fusion with the plastron are discernible.

The basic internal arrangement of the scutes on the carapace was established. Four, occasionally five, vertebral scutes, bordered by five matching costals on each side, are readily evident. Around the borders of the carapace, however, there were large numbers of scutes, corresponding to the marginals seen in contemporary chelonians. These were augmented with both supramarginal and inframarginal scutes. A regular pattern of scutes on the plastron had already developed by this stage. The intergular scute, at the cranial end of the shell, along with both caudal and intercaudal scutes, are all discernible.

These early turtles are grouped in the super-family Proganochelyidea, which is usually split into two families on the basis of the arrangement of the pelvis, relative to the plastron. Fusion has taken place in the case of the Proganochelyidea, whereas this development is not discernible in the case of the Proterochersidae. These chelonians appear to have been of moderate dimensions, with *Proganochelys* itself being about 30 cm (2 ft) in over-all length, while *Proterochersis* was smaller, being approximately half this size.

The Jurassic Period

The continuing evolution of chelonians is clearly apparent through the Jurassic Period, which lasted about 60 million years. They began to colonise the world's oceans, and had also spread into the present-day continents of North America and Asia. The major group through this period continued to be members of the now extinct sub-order Amphichelydia. Several significant changes can be seen by a study of their fossilised remains. They had lost the teeth present in the jaws of their Triassic ancestors, while the sides of the plastron now reached up to the carapace, increasing the protection afforded by the shell. The ribs had now been fully incorporated into the structure of the shell and, in some cases, the pubis was linked to the plastron. At this stage, however, none of these chelonians could retract their head or limbs into their shells, and thus must have been quite vulnerable to predators. Perhaps not surprisingly, they did not venture permanently onto land, but remained close to water, even when they were breeding.

At the beginning of the Jurassic Period, the world appears to have been relatively cold, but then the climate gradually warmed up. Contemporary Europe was an area of tropical islands set in a coral sea. Certainly, by this period, marine turtles were established, and they would doubtless have come ashore to nest like present-day species. Indeed, members of the family Thalassemydidae shared some characteristics with modern sea turtles, such as fontanelles, gaps in the bony shell which would normally ossify early in life in most creatures, but actually remain open throughout the reptile's life. At least 11 members of this family are known to have occurred, and a closely related group, the

Aperotemporalidae, also roamed the oceans during this period. These turtles are less well known from fossilised remains.

The amphichelydians collectively mark a significant stage in the development of chelonians, as, during the Jurassic Period, the forerunners of the contemporary sub-order Cryptodira emerged. Today, this is the predominant grouping, in which all but two of 13 extant families are classified. Cryptodiran chelonians are sometimes described as the hidden-neck turtles, because they draw their head back into the shell in a vertical movement. The cervical vertebrae in the neck region are sufficiently flexible to create a sigmoid curve for this purpose. The actual shape of the vertebrae have become modified as a result, being simplified in structure. The transverse processes, located horizontally on each side of the individual vertebrae, are greatly reduced in size, while the dorsal spines are similarly less prominent. The flexibility of this part of the backbone is increased to facilitate movement.

The Cretaceous Period

The other sub-order recognised today, the Pleurodira, did not evolve until the Cretaceous Period. This appears somewhat anomalous, however, as the pleurodirans are usually considered less advanced in evolutionary terms. Unlike their cryptodiran ancestors, they curl their head back into the shell by means of a horizontal rather than vertical movement. Their neck is curled to the side during this manoeuvre, and these chelonians are often described, accordingly, as side-necked turtles. The modifications to the shape of the cervical vertebrae, seen in the cryptodirans, are effectively reversed in this sub-order. Indeed, the dorsal spines, especially on the posterior cervical vertebrae, are prominent, as are the transverse processes. A further point of distinction in the case of side-necked chelonians is that the pelvic girdle is joined to the shell.

Marine species appear to have thrived during the Cretaceous Period, along with other sea-dwelling reptiles, such as the plesiosaurs and ichthyosaurs. The oceans continued to encroach on the land, but, more significantly, this period also saw a dramatic increase in the numbers of teleost fishes. This clearly favoured the development of predatory creatures, which would feed not only on the fish, but also on other marine occupants.

Fearsome hunters, including the large lizard-like mosasaurs, roamed the oceans at this stage, but size could, in turn, prove a deterrent to such predators. *Archelon* was a huge turtle which lived alongside these other reptilian groups, protected by its huge shell, which could be as large as 3.6 m (12 ft) at its longest point. The hooked beak-like tip to its upper jaw may have enabled *Archelon* to grab fish more effectively, as it had lost the low, elongated teeth seen in earlier chelonians.

Marine turtles appear to have reached their greatest diversity during this period. It is known that there were at least 15 genera present in the seas of the Cretaceous Period. Contemporary with *Archelon* were members of the *Caretta* and *Chelonia* genera, which are still represented in the oceans today, about 100 million years later. Now, however, only nine species remain in total, and *Archelon*, as well as other genera, appears to have vanished without leaving any descendants.

A number of reports of giant sea turtles, apparently significantly larger than known species, do exist, however, and it is not impossible that a small population, breeding on an uninhabited group of islands, could have remained undetected. Several interesting references to giant turtles can be found in ancient literature, describing such creatures from the Indian Ocean. Aelian, writing in the third century AD, refers to huge turtles whose shells could be approximately 7.2 m (24 ft) in circumference. These were used as roofing material by the local people, and were thus unlikely to have been brittle fossils.

During the Middle Ages, Al Edrisi described such turtles as occurring to the west of present-day Sri Lanka, and growing to a length approaching 9 m (30 ft). In Sumatran legend, this giant chelonian is described as the 'father of all turtles'. If such creatures do inhabit the world's oceans, they would have to be pelagic, living in the open sea. Here, they are most likely to have escaped the attention of zoologists down the centuries. In contrast, at least some of the marine chelonians of the Cretaceous Period appear not to have ventured far from the shoreline.

The close of the Cretaceous Period

The events which led to the extinction of the dinosaurs and many other creatures at the end of the Cretaceous Period also affected chelonians, although they survived this phase better than any other reptilian group. Fifteen recognised families existed in the late Cretaceous Period, and certainly eight of these survived into the Tertiary.

As to why so many lifeforms, ranging from huge dinosaurs to the ammonites of the oceans, died out at the close of the Cretaceous Period, has never been satisfactorily explained. It seems likely that climatic changes may well have been the most significant factor in their demise. Chelonians probably survived this period because they were less sensitive to temperature shifts than other reptiles, notably the dinosaurs. Like the crocodilians, which also emerged into the Tertiary Period, chelonians were able to hibernate in their environment, and could therefore withstand cooler conditions for a period.

Increasing seasonal temperature differentials would not necessarily have been a serious handicap to these reptiles, within certain limits. When the temperature rose again, they could re-emerge from their temporary slumber and feed, with breeding also taking place during this warmer phase. The eggs themselves may have effectively overwintered, hatching at the onset of warmer conditions, like those of some contemporary chelonians in temperate areas. In addition, their omnivorous feeding habits meant that they could adapt more easily to the corresponding changes in vegetation than the herbivorous dinosaurs and the carnivorous species which preyed upon them. Their body fat would nurture them over colder periods, as with hibernating chelonians today.

Two families of chelonians vanished quite early during the succeeding Eocene era, approximately 60 million years ago, but the general adaptability of these reptiles soon saw the emergence of new families. These appear to have directly replaced those which became extinct, ensuring the continued widespread distribution of chelonians as a group right down to the present day. Some contemporary families of aquatic turtles, such as the soft-shelled group, Trionychidae, had developed during the Cretaceous Period, while the Eocene saw the emergence of emydid chelonians.

Steps onto land

This family, Emydidae, is now the largest extant group, with representative species occurring in the Americas, Africa and Eurasia. Forerunners of today's genera, such as *Echmatemys* in North America, were established by this stage. These particular chelonians are believed to be the ancestors of the genus *Trachemys*, with the earliest forms of this genus having evolved by the Eocene era. These chelonians were probably like the contemporary *T. scripta* group, of which the red-eared slider (*T. scripta elegans*) is now perhaps best known through its popularity as a pet.

Some species in this family were larger in size in the past than they are today. A sub-species of the common box turtle (*Terrapene carolina putnami*), which appears to have ranged through central and southern areas of the United States, could attain a carapace length of 30 cm (1 ft), measured across the centre of the top of the shell in a straight line. It was obviously closely related to the Gulf Coast box turtle (*T. c. major*), which is not only the largest surviving sub-species, growing to just over 20 cm (8 in), but also has noticeably flared marginal shields around the rear of the carapace, like its extinct relative.

However, these box turtles would have been dwarfed by the members of the genus *Broilia*, which occurred somewhat later, during the subsequent Oligocene Period, in France. Cartilaginous attachments on each side of the shell joined the carapace to the plastron, forming a flexible link on both sides of the body. *Broilia* species were large emydids, and could grow to over 75 cm (30 in). They had rather domed shells, like some present-day members of this family, which are semi-terrestrial in their habits.

It seems likely that the true land tortoises, forming the family Testudinidae, may well have evolved from earlier emydid stock of this type. The first known fossilised remains of tortoises actually date back to the Eocene Period. There is some evidence to suggest that terrestrial chelonians may have been in existence by the end of the Cretaceous Period, however, in the form of the dermatemyid species, named *Zangerlia testudinimorpha*, which has been discovered in Mongolia. Some features, such as the shape of the humerus, are more indicative of aquatic chelonians, so this may have been an ancestral form, rather than a truly terrestrial species itself.

Land tortoises

The fossil history of the Testudinidae suggests that the family arose either in North America or Africa, as it is here that the earliest definite remains have been unearthed. These tortoises appear to have resembled the Burmese tortoise (*Geochelone emys*), a forest-dwelling species found in parts of Asia today. They were of medium size, and initially had a relatively flat shell, reflecting their aquatic ancestry. This became modified, in the case of the carapace, to form a domed covering over the top of the body. The raised shell would doubtless have afforded better protection against faster and more agile predators, who otherwise might well have been able to crush the unfortunate reptile in their jaws. In aquatic species, streamlining is a more effective defence, as it lowers water resistance and enables the chelonian to swim quickly away from danger.

The raised shell of terrestrial chelonians is also physiologically valuable, as it provides for an increased lung capacity. Indeed, tortoises have proportionately bigger lungs than emydid turtles of similar size, with the notable exception of the box turtles of the genus *Terrapene*, which live primarily on land. The reversion to a flatter shell profile in some modern tortoises, notably the pancake tortoise (*Malacochersus tornieri*), is a relatively recent occurrence. It has enabled this species to adapt to a particular environment, hiding under rocks where a domed shell would prove a significant handicap. Pancake tortoises are also very agile, and are able to climb and move at speed.

While the early tortoises wandered through the tropical forests which existed during the Eocene Period, feeding on fallen fruit, their modern relatives have adapted to a much wider range of habitats. A number of species inhabit arid areas of grassland, and also occur in sub-tropical regions. The gait of the tortoise has altered as evolution has proceeded, so that the more advanced species, such as the African hingebacks

Plate 52   The gait of tortoises can vary noticeably. The hingebacks (*Kinixys* spp), for example, have a very upright gait, described as digitigrade, compared with other species such as the Mediterranean spur-thighed tortoise (*Testudo graeca*).

(*Kinixys* spp), walk in a digitigrade manner, using only their toes for this purpose, rather than the whole of the feet. Changes in the limb bones also occurred to assist with locomotion on land, although the pelvis is not significantly modified from that of the emydids.

Over 200 species of land tortoises are believed to have existed, of which 30 still survive. It has been possible, in some cases, to trace the development of some early species through their fossilised remains. The Eocene sub-genus *Manouria* was probably the ancestral form of the often heavily armoured *Hesperotestudo*. Members of this sub-genus have been discovered, primarily in North America, and it was here that these species appear to have divided into two distinct forms. One group retained a heavy shell with a sculptured outline, while the other developed a lighter body casing with smooth edges.

Approximately 23 species of *Hesperotestudo* have been discovered, and the most recent, in geological terms, was *Geochelone (Hesperotestudo) wilsoni*, which survived from the Pleistocene Period into the Quaternary. These tortoises inhabited eastern parts of the United States, and were of the thick-shelled form. They appear to have died out, possibly because of climatic changes, without leaving any descendants.

Another well-protected group of tortoises, also occurring in North America, has been classified in the sub-genus *Caudochelys*. The remains of nine distinct species are known and, tracing their fossil history, it is clear that these chelonians became larger in size as they evolved from the latter part of the Eocene Period through to the Pleistocene. One of the most recent species was *Geochelone (Caudochelys) crassiscutata*, which lived from the middle part of the Pleistocene to the close of that period, and had a shell which was at least 120 cm (4 ft) in overall length.

The only surviving land tortoises in North America today are the four species forming the genus *Gopherus*. Fossil evidence suggests that they could be descended from the Oligocene species, named *Stylemys nebrascensis*. Other *Stylemys* tortoises, extending into the Miocene era, have been found in North America, and apparent representatives of the genus have also been discovered in both France and the USSR. Several anatomical features are suggestive of the link with *Gopherus*, notably the presence of a premaxillary ridge on the skull. But *Stylemys nebrascensis* was certainly a fairly primitive form, lacking the typical pattern of octagonal and quadrilateral neural bones. Nor is the usual contraction and expansion, as seen in the pleural bones of modern chelonians, contributing to the dome-like shape of the carapace, apparent in this species of *Stylemys*. Signs of this modification can be detected, however, in other fossilised remains of the genus.

The genus *Geochelone*, which is still widely distributed today, has already been mentioned through various sub-genera, of which 12 are recognised, half of which are no longer extant. In the Americas, the genus has suffered a significant decrease in range, probably largely because of climatic changes which occurred during the Pleistocene era. It is now confined to parts of Central and South America, as well as the Galapagos Islands. Four species still survive, but only the Chilean tortoise (*Geochelone chilensis*) appears with certainty in the fossil record. Its ancestor, *Geochelone (Chelonoidis) gringorum*, has been discovered in Miocene deposits in Argentina, with *chilensis* itself first occurring with certainty during the Pleistocene era.

Geochelone (Chelonoidis) hesterna, the shell and part of a skeleton of which were discovered in Colombia and first reported during 1971, was also a Miocene species. This may have been the ancestral form of both the red-footed and yellow-footed tortoises (*G. carbonaria* and *G. denticulata*), although it appears to have been more reminiscent of the latter.

Land giants

Six species in this particular sub-genus are known only from fossilised evidence, including large tortoises which occurred on Caribbean islands, such as *Geochelone (Chelonoidis) cubensis*, a late Pleistocene example from the island of Cuba. Giant *Geochelone* tortoises can still be found on the Galapagos Island, off the coast of Ecuador, where *G. elephantopus* still roams.

The genus is also present in the Old World, and similar large tortoises, forming the species *G. gigantea*, can be found on the Aldabran Islands in the Indian Ocean. However, both these forms would have been dwarfed by the biggest land tortoise yet discovered. *Geochelone (Megalochelys) sivalensis* (sometimes described as *Colossochelys atlas*), occurred through the Pleistocene Period. It appears to have been a widely distributed Asiatic species, as its remains have been discovered in both India and Burma and further east, on the islands of Sulawesi, Java and Timor.

The actual size of this huge tortoise has been the subject of controversy since its discovery in 1835, but initial estimates of a shell size of 3.6 m (12 ft) are now accepted as being excessive. It was probably between 1.8 and 2.4 m (6–8 ft) over all. A similar, but slightly smaller giant, classified as *Geochelone (Megalochelys) cautleyi*, may have occurred in India at the same time as its relative. There is also a possibility that they could even have been the same species, as the fossilised remains of *cautleyi* are very incomplete. Certainly, however, another distinctive member of this sub-genus inhabited Mauritius, which is quite close to the range of the Aldabran giant tortoise (*G. gigantea*) today.

Testudo species

The other major Old World genus of tortoises which is still extant, known as *Testudo*, had evolved by the Eocene. Early remains from this period have been discovered in France, where both *Testudo corroyi* and *Testudo doduni* occurred at this time. The emergence of the two tortoises, widely kept as pets in Europe, appears to have been a relatively recent development, which took place as late as the Pleistocene era. The Mediterranean spur-thighed tortoise (*T. graeca*) had an equally wide range then, as fossilised evidence found on opposite sides of the Mediterranean

Sea, in both France and Morocco, has confirmed. Hermann's tortoise (*T. hermanni*) was confined to Eurasia, as it is today, and its remains have been discovered in Italy in Pleistocene deposits.

The distribution of *Testudo* tortoises used to extend further eastwards than is presently the case, with species being known to have occurred through the USSR into China. Several shells and a complete specimen have been found in this latter country, dating from the Pliocene era. These tortoises also ranged further into northern Europe in the past, with the remains of one species, named *Testudo comptoni*, having been unearthed on the Isle of Sheppey, close to London, England. This dates back to the early part of the Eocene Period.

Horned giants: the meiolaniids

The most bizarre group of tortoises yet discovered are the members of the family Meiolaniidae. They probably evolved during the late Cretaceous Period, with the remains of the earliest genera being found in Argentina. Later representatives of the family have been discovered in south-eastern Australia, as well as on Lord Howe Island to the east, and neighbouring Walpole Island, close to New Caledonia. No land tortoises now survive in Australia, although the meiolaniids appear to have lived until quite recently, certainly on Lord Howe Island.

Fossilised evidence confirms that this group of chelonians could grow to a large size, and had an unmistakable appearance, with horns extending almost horizontally from the sides of their heads. These horns could be as much as 60 cm (2 ft) apart. The actual shape of the horns varied among the different genera, and they were quite short in the case of the earliest examples, such as *Crossochelys*. The skulls of these tortoises were quite large and, apart from the horns, meiolaniids were also protected by having their tails covered with bony armour. The reasons underlying the development of the unique horns are unclear, but when considered with the tail, they may have offered protection against potential predators.

The relationships of this group of tortoises are equally obscure. It has been suggested that they could have been pleurodires, but their pelvis was not fused with the shell. In spite of this fact, however, the horizontal processes of the cervical vertebrae are clearly evident, and this feature is, of course, considered to be a pleurodiran characteristic. Because of the unusual shape of the head, however, these lateral processes may well have developed in an atypical fashion simply to support the increased weight resulting from the horns and accompanying musculature. As a result, more recent opinion suggests that meiolaniids were actually atypical cryptodires.

The family vanished from South America at the start of the Tertiary era, and yet survived almost to the present day in Australia. Here, in the absence of predatory mammalian species, it now seems more likely that climatic changes, or indeed the spread of early humans, accompanied by dingoes, may have contributed to the demise of the meiolaniids. The last remains of this family from Lord Howe Island are probably no more than 120,000 years old. Yet the island now gives little indication of its past suitability for a population of tortoises, and two factors may have been involved in their extinction. Firstly, a rise in sea level would have destroyed much of the suitable available habitat, leaving just the steep slopes of the island protruding from the ocean. Perhaps more significantly, climatic changes would have interfered with the metabolism of the tortoises. Not only would eggs have failed to hatch, but males may well have become sub-fertile under such conditions, if studies involving contemporary chelonians can be applied to the meiolaniids. Certainly, the climate on Lord Howe Island today is like that of northern Europe, with the maximum temperature, even during the summer, unlikely to exceed 26°C (79°F).

Movements and migrations

These separate South American and Australasian populations could, of course, have evolved on similar lines from different ancestral stock, but close study of the anatomy of the known genera has effectively ruled out this possibility. It therefore means that they must have spread to Australasia from South America, where the earliest fossils of the family have been discovered.

A map of the world today suggests that the most obvious means of migration would have to be across the oceans, either in an eastward or westward direction. Since remains of meiolaniids have only been found in eastern Australia, this might indicate that their ancestors travelled across the Pacific Ocean from the western seaboard of South America.

At this stage, however, this continent lay closer to Africa, increasing the distance required to make a successful landing in Australia. Conversely, if meiolaniids had taken the eastward sea route, it is likely that they would have come into contact with land at the tip of present-day South Africa, as the area of ocean separating southern Africa from Antarctica was then greatly decreased. No remains of the family have ever been found in this area, or indeed, anywhere else on this route. A further drawback to this theory is that it implies that the meiolaniids were most likely to have arrived in Western Australia, where the group is also unknown. As the centre of Australia is believed to have been initially a sea, and then a desert, it seems less likely that the meiolaniids would immediately have continued eastwards.

The key to their distribution, therefore, appears to lie in the southerly continent of Antarctica, which formerly lay further north. Instead of being a frozen wasteland, Antarctica then acted as a land-bridge, connected to both South America and Australia. Even as the land masses of the old continents of Laurasia and Gondwanaland broke up, so it is more likely that tortoises could have drifted the relatively short distance to Antarctica, and journeyed from here, rather than bobbing across the Pacific Ocean. A land-bridge would have enabled them to enter eastern Australia directly, rather than having to undergo a further trans-continental migration across a sea or desert.

Additional support for this theory comes from the presence of two members of the family Chelidae, which occur in Western Australia today. This is another family found in South America, and it almost certainly relied upon a land-bridge to expand its range, crossing as early as the Cretaceous Period. Furthermore, fossilised evidence of the presence of chelonians in Antarctica has been discovered, and this dates back to the Miocene Period when the land was obviously much warmer than it is today.

Contemporary distribution patterns

No clear parallels can be drawn between the spread of the meiolaniids and the colonisation of the Galapagos Islands by another South American genus, *Geochelone*. These islands are of recent volcanic origin, probably less than five million years old, and the length of time that they have been populated by tortoises is unclear. Certainly, the volcanic lava would need to have been colonised previously by plants if the tortoises were to be able to survive successfully here.

It is almost certain, therefore, that the tortoises drifted to the Galapagos Islands, as these emerged from the ocean bed, rather than having been previously joined to an existing land mass. The ancestral form of the Galapagos tortoises is unclear, but it seems likely that this *Geochelone* species was itself relatively large. Certainly, there were big tortoises of this genus already in existence throughout the Americas by this stage, having been discovered in California and Colombia, for example. Ocean currents are subject to change, of course, but it seems more likely that tortoises which reached the Galapagos would have come from further north, carried southwards to the islands, having perhaps originated in middle America. Their likelihood of survival would probably have been greater in these warmer currents than those coming up from the south.

The tortoises may not even have been submerged in the sea, however, but could have been transported, at least for some of the journey, on beds of vegetation, possibly washed out to sea on rivers full of flood water. Large tortoises would probably have been better equipped to survive an arduous journey of this type, in view of their great bulk, and could certainly have drifted for a month or so in this way without coming to obvious harm. It has been estimated that just one successful crossing every 100,000 years could have ensured the successful colonisation of the islands. Once washed onto the shore, however, there were further barriers to be crossed before the tortoise could eat again after its enforced fast.

One significant biological factor, which could have favoured the successful colonisation of islands by individual chelonians, may well have been the ability of females to lay several successive clutches of fertile eggs following one successful mating. A female which was able to reproduce by this means would, at least in theory, be able to establish a viable population in a given area by herself. Male hatchlings would then ensure the continuance of the species, by mating with their siblings.

Although the early meiolaniids probably did not rely on rafting to reach Australia, this may, in turn, have facilitated their colonisation of Lord Howe and Walpole Islands. Certainly, the movement of these chelonians to the former locality occurred after they were established in Australia. Lord Howe Island is also volcanic in origin, like the Galapagos, and first erupted from the sea about seven million years ago.

The *Geochelone* species present in South America probably came themselves originally from Africa, although the route they took is unclear. If it was by direct migration, this would need to have taken place during the Cretaceous Period, before the continents separated. At this stage, however, land tortoises were only just emerging as a group, and there is no fossil evidence to support early colonisation of South America. Instead, it seems likely that they crossed the Atlantic Ocean directly, with the highest proportion of fossil species being found to date on the southern part of the continent. This tends to suggest that the early development occurred here, with the species radiating northwards.

In contrast, the fresh-water chelonians appear to have entered South America via Central America, with the highest diversity of species being found in Colombia, the country which joins directly with the Panamanian land-bridge. This movement probably occurred after the Pliocene Period, once the land masses had joined together. It is clear that some northern species have migrated a considerable distance southwards, and altered somewhat in isolation. The black-bellied slider is often classified as the most southerly race of the well-known North American species *Trachemys scripta*, ranging into Uruguay and Argentina. Its presence here is something of a mystery, however, as *T. dorbignyi* is well separated from other sub-species.

The spread of fresh-water turtles is actually more dependent on land than water. Unlike their terrestrial counterparts, they are far less able to survive periods of dehydration and are thus rendered much more vulnerable to the effects of salt water. Whereas a tortoise will float, bobbing passively along on top of the waves, a fresh-water turtle will become immersed in the salty environment, sinking readily or else expending considerable effort to remain at the surface.

Certain species, such as members of the *Trachemys* group, are better able to survive limited exposure to salt water than others, primarily because their skin is less permeable. Osmosis would otherwise ensure a rapid and lethal loss of water from the body. It seems likely that the colonisation of certain Caribbean islands by *Trachemys* species was directly achieved by turtles from the American mainland. These could have drifted, or even been rafted until they reached land. There are accounts of rafts of vegetation carrying such turtles, at least from island to island.

Human involvement

The most recent means of the spread of chelonians has resulted from human involvement. Particularly during the last century, when the

Plate 53   A yellow-footed tortoise (*Geochelone denticulata*) – this South American species is still widely hunted for food throughout its range. Chelonians are obviously much easier to catch than other potential sources of meat, which renders them highly vulnerable to human persecution.

potentially disastrous effects of such introductions on existing ecosystems were not fully appreciated, it became fashionable to move exotic creatures and try to establish them in new environments. Indeed, several attempts were made to set up populations of the European pond turtle (*Emys orbicularis*) in England at this stage. This species had, in fact, been native in the UK about 5,000 years ago, but presumably died out because of climatic changes. Its distribution now extends as far as northern parts of Germany and central France.

Although the attempted reintroduction of these turtles was unsuccessful, it seems likely that some of the contemporary Caribbean populations of *Trachemys* were achieved in this way. The red-eared turtle (*T. s. elegans*) appears to have been established successfully on Guadeloupe and some islands of the Bahamas group by this means. Other likely introductions are the presence of the Cuban slider (*T. decussata*) on the island of Marie

Galante, in the French West Indies, while those on Cayman Brac are said to be the descendants of a pair of turtles released there during 1875. Aside from human involvement, however, further spread in this region could conceivably be achieved by rafting, assuming that the islands themselves would be favourable for colonisation. This does not appear to be the case in every instance. Following the known rafting of *Trachemys* from Puerto Rico to nearby Vieques Island, for example, colonisation here has proved a failure in the absence of established areas of fresh water.

In the same way that turtles were brought to the Caribbean by humans, so populations of red-footed tortoises (*Geochelone carbonaria*) have also been established on many islands. They include a group on the island of St Kitts, inhabiting the old volcanic crater of Mount Misery. Elsewhere, it is possible that the populations of Celebes tortoise (*Geochelone 'forsteni'*), found on the islands of Sulawesi and Halmahera, off the coast of Asia, may have been introduced, but the precise origins of this species are obscure. Certainly, these tortoises are very similar to the mainland species known as the Travancore tortoise (*Geochelone travancorica*). Early Hindu travellers may have been responsible for the introduction of these tortoises from India.

The translocation and introduction of tortoises to new safe refuges in the future may also have to be undertaken, to ensure the survival of some species, relying possibly on captive-bred stock for this purpose. Indeed, the impact of the human population, and resulting environmental changes, from drainage of marshland and felling of forests to the pollution of waterways, pose probably a greater threat to the continued survival of chelonians than any other that they have previously faced during their long history on this planet.

Chapter 5
The Chelonian Families

The order Chelonia comprises two sub-orders, of which the cryptodira is the largest, comprising all but two of the 13 recognised familes. The pleurodires, or side-necks, constitute the other sub-order, being clearly distinguishable by the way that they curl their neck into an S-shaped configuration when retracting their heads back into their shells.

This part of the book reviews all the families, and both the genera and species within these groupings. The classification of chelonians does not differ from that of other animals, operating through a series of ranks down to sub-specific level, when only minor differences separate the populations in question. Classification is always subject to revision, as new anatomical, behavioural or physiological factors of significance become known. This accounts for differences in the classificatory position of some chelonians, although usually the higher ranks are unaffected to any noticeable extent. More disagreement among taxonomists exists about the lower ranks, especially as to whether sub-specific status is merited. In order to show how the system operates, the leopard tortoise (*Geochelone pardalis*) is shown as an example below:

Order: Chelonia
   Sub-order: Cryptodira
Family: Testudinidae
Genus: *Geochelone*
   Sub-genus: (*Geochelone*)
Species: *Geochelone (Geochelone) pardalis*
   Sub-species: *Geochelone (Geochelone) pardalis pardalis*
                Geochelone (Geochelone) pardalis babcocki

In many cases, no distinctive sub-genus is recognised and this is then dropped from the classificatory breakdown. The sub-species where the species' description is repeated is known as the nominate form. Then a name and date shown in parenthesis indicate when the species, or sub-species as appropriate, was first described. The use of parenthesis around this information confirms that the classificatory position of the taxon concerned has been altered since it was first ascribed to the appropriate category. Only names from the rank of genus downwards are written in italics. This helps to establish the actual status of the term being used. The classificatory position used here is based on that adopted by Pritchard (1979) and Iverson (1986) with slight modifications.

Sub-order: Cryptodira

Family: Carettochelydiae – Fly River Turtle

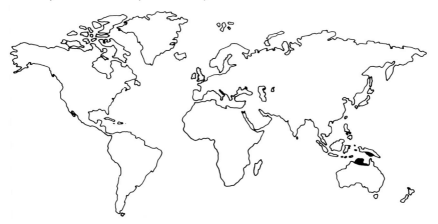

Map 1   Distribution of the family Carettochelyidae.

Members of this family used to have a much wider distribution in the past. Their remains have been unearthed in Europe, where they died out during the Oligocene Period, about 28 million years ago, as well as in parts of North America and Asia. Today, only one species still survives, being confined to southern New Guinea, in the vicinity of the Fly River, and also apparently in a separate locality surrounding the Daly River in Australia. This site, in the Northern Territory, occurs about 160 km (100 miles) to the south-west of the town of Darwin.

The species itself (*Carettochelys insculpta*) is known under a variety of different common names. These include Fly River turtle, pitted-shell turtle, pig-nosed soft-shell turtle and, perhaps most correctly from an anatomical viewpoint, the New Guinea plateless turtle. In fact, it shows a number of similarities with marine species, especially with regard to its feet. These are much more like the flippers of sea turtles, also showing the characteristic reduction in the number of claws, than those of other fresh-water species.

Although it lacks scutes, the carapace being covered instead by a layer of skin, this is not actually a soft-shell turtle. There is, for example, no reduction in the bone structure of the plastron, which remains rigid, and the central opening associated with soft-shells is not apparent in this species. The unusual wrinkled appearance of the carapace gave rise to the species name of *insculpta*. These turtles are greyish in colour, with a paler plastron. Their skin has a pitted appearance, while their unusual nose is rather like the snout of a pig, as one of the common names suggests. The long nose is probably an adaptation to enable it to remain submerged for most of the time. When breathing by this means, the turtle just breaks the surface of the water to obtain air. Pharyngeal and cloacal respiration appear highly significant in the case of this species.

These turtles are virtually unique in showing slight movements in the actual vicinity of the chest when they breathe. This is related to the structure of the shell, notably the plastron, where rather than being rigidly fused together, certain of the bony plates are held together by cartilage, instead of bone. The bridges at the sides of the shell are also relatively weak. This characteristic is shared with marine species, emphasising the close relationship which exists between these chelonians.

It appears that the Fly River turtle is omnivorous in its feeding habits, taking crustaceans and fish, as well as vegetable matter. They will also eat fruit, and captive individuals are said to show a preference for pears.

The natives of the Kiwai tribe consider the species sacred, in spite of increasing pressure to hunt it for food. They relate how these turtles, lying side by side in the mud, showed them how to copulate. Before this time, the tribe had comprised men only, with women being used only as servants, having been captured from other tribes. Local superstition holds that killing a *minorva*, as these turtles are known, will result in impotency.

The breeding period of *Carettochelys* takes place during the dry season, when the sandbanks are uncovered. This period extends from September to November in Papua New Guinea. The eggs are hard-shelled and spherical in shape, with a normal clutch comprising 15 to 20, although large numbers up to 27 have been recorded. Only a shallow nest is dug, in contrast to the deeper nesting chambers of marine species.

When they hatch, the young turtles are just over 5 cm (2 in) in length, and differ somewhat from the adults in terms of their appearance. The carapace has serrated edges and, in a few cases, some traces of scutes may be apparent at this stage. The highly aquatic nature of this species is clearly evident in the paddle-like structure of the hatchlings' limbs. When adult, the young turtles can grow to a carapace size of just under 50 cm (20 in) and weigh over 15 kg (35 lb).

The presence of the population in northern Australia, apparently only discovered as recently as 1969, is mysterious. It could have been introduced, either by direct movement or by migration across the Arafura Sea from Papua New Guinea. There is little doubt that these turtles would be able to swim well in the sea, sharing various critical features with marine species, so this explanation is not totally without foundation. It seems less likely that movement occurred in the reverse direction.

Although its habits are not well known in the wild, the species appears to be quite common in the rivers in the south of Papua New Guinea, and also extends to Lake Jamoer. Their growth rate appears slow, based on the very few individuals which have been kept in zoos. One, obtained as a youngster, has lived at the Bronx Zoo in New York for 20 years.

Family: Chelydridae – Snapping Turtles

These large fresh-water turtles tend to be aggressive, as their name suggests. Their distribution extends from parts of southern Canada into the eastern United States, with a line between central Montana and

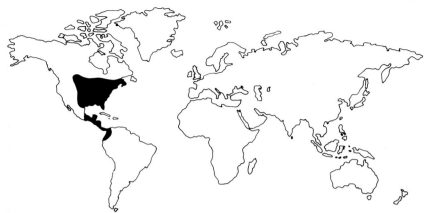

Map 2   Distribution of the family Chelydridae.

eastern New Mexico marking the westerly extent of the species' spread. Sub-species also occur further south, in Mexico and other Central American countries. The common snapping turtle (*Chelydra serpentina*) is more commonly encountered than the alligator snapping turtle (*Macroclemys temmincki*). The clear distinguishing feature between the two species is the appearance of the carapace. In the case of the alligator snapping turtle, there are highly evident keels, forming distinct ridges similar to those seen on the backs of alligators. It tends to be more sedentary in its habits.

The common snapping turtle, in contrast, is an aggressive predator with large, powerful jaws which can cut through flesh with devastating

Plate 54   The common snapping turtle (*Chelydra serpentina*) is a large and predatory fresh-water species, with a smooth carapace distinguishing it from the related alligator snapping turtle (*Macroclemys temmincki*).

effect. Large individuals are known to have caused injury to people unwary enough to step into or swim in the water near them, and they are quite capable of removing a toe or finger if given the opportunity. The enlargement of the head, presumably to facilitate such predation, has meant that it cannot be retracted into the shell. Cartilaginous bridges attach the plastron to the relatively thin carapace. The rapid darting head movements of this otherwise sluggish species result from the curvature of the ribs close to the vertebral column, which are directed away from the inner surface of the carapace. This has enabled development of the musculature necessary for striking rapidly with the head.

Four sub-species of the common snapping turtle are usually recognised, of which the Floridan race (*C. s. osceola*) is one of the most distinctive. It possesses a relatively large number of swellings around its neck and adjoining parts of the body. The function of these is unclear, although it has been suggested that they could be useful for the purpose of gaseous exchange. The papillae increase the surface area of the skin, and could therefore produce an increase in gaseous transfer.

The common snapping turtle is a particularly hardy chelonian, and fears have recently been expressed about the possibilities of the species establishing itself in Britain. Hatchlings are sometimes imported via the pet trade, and it has been suggested that these, if liberated into suitable waters, could establish a breeding population. This seems a remote possibility, however, and any release of this type would be a direct contravention of the existing Wildlife and Countryside Act 1981, which forbids the deliberate liberation of non-native species. While common snappers may be able to survive in the wild, at least for a limited period, in the British climate, their eggs are likely to be less viable, so that a major population spread would be unlikely.

For much of the time, these turtles remain submerged, although on occasions they may emerge to bask on land. They do not favour fast-flowing rivers, preferring instead quiet stretches of water or lakes. The size of these turtles has always been the subject of much interest. They can grow well in excess of 30 cm (1 ft), and the largest carapace length yet measured has been 46.25 cm (18½ in). Their weight is clearly influenced by food intake, and captive specimens can become relatively obese, weighing up to 39 kg (86 lb) or so. Males tend to grow to a larger size than females. They can also be distinguished by the relative positions of the cloacal openings, that of the male being further from the base of the tail. The plastron of males tends to show a greater reduction in size, which may facilitate mating.

It is the alligator snapping turtle which is the giant of the family, however, with males again growing to a much larger size than females. Their carapace can be over 75 cm (30 in) in length, with the skull alone being nearly 25 cm (10 in) across. Individuals weighing over 90 kg (200 lb) are not unknown, making this species one of the biggest forms of fresh-water chelonian. In the case of the alligator snapping turtle, these giants appear most commonly on the northern edge of its distribution, where the species is only rarely encountered. It has been suggested that these are very old individuals, leading solitary lives, and possibly not even breeding in this area.

Reports of significantly bigger snappers than those already documented have yet to be verified. One, christened the 'Beast of Busco', inhabited Fulk's Lake, close to the town of Churubusco in the state of Indiana. It was first seen by a farmer during the summer of 1948, and reappeared during the following March. Eye-witness accounts describe this snapper as being about the size of a dining-room table, and covered in algae. Its weight was estimated to be around 227 kg (500 lb).

Attempts to catch this monster followed, and on 12 March, a stockade of stakes was set up around the turtle, which was submerged in about 6 m (20 ft) of water. It broke out of the enclosure, however, and subsequently escaped numerous attempts, ranging from the bizarre to the ridiculous, to recapture it. Finally, an attempt was made to drain the lake, but this failed, as the crater itself was a deep glacial hollow. After two hunters almost died in the resulting treacherous band of mud around the lake, interest in this alligator snapping turtle waned, and whether it still survives is unknown.

The range of this species has contracted, and it is now concentrated in the drainage channels of the Mississippi River. It used to extend further to the north west, and a now extinct species, *Macrochelys schmidti*, lived in southern Dakota during the Miocene Period, about 26 million years ago. Remains of similar turtles have also been unearthed in Europe, proving that this family had a much wider distribution in the past.

The power of the jaws of the alligator snapper has become part of American folklore, with stories being told of how these chelonians can shatter a broomstick in their mouths. It seems that these may be exaggerated; individuals weighing up to 18 kg (40 lb) would have difficulty in splitting even a pencil in two.

The alligator snapping turtle is a relatively sedate predator, luring fish and other prey into its mouth. This is achieved by the presence of a fleshy lure which resembles a worm in appearance. This can be moved, creating an even more lifelike impression. As soon as the prey is safely within the mouth, the turtle clamps its jaws shut. Snappers do not feed exclusively on live food, however, and are capable scavengers, apparently possessing a keen sense of smell.

One individual was trained by an Indian in Indiana to locate the bodies of drowned people in the waterways. The turtle, tied to a wire leash, was released into the water from a boat, and then, by tracking the wire, the body would invariably be found. Handling these large turtles is potentially dangerous, because of their quick movements, but grasping the carapace, fore and aft, offers the safest means.

Family: Dermatemydidae – Central American River Turtle

The only member of this family occurs in Central America, ranging from Mexico southwards to parts of Honduras. Known scientifically as *Der-*

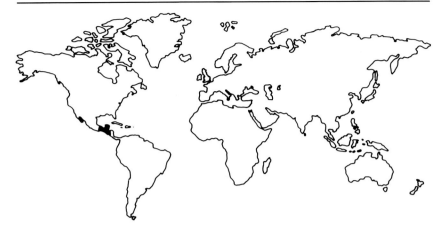

Map 3   Distribution of the family Dermatemydidae.

matemys mawri, this species is also called the Tabasco turtle, after the Mexican state where it was first discovered in 1847. It appears to be the only remaining member of an ancient group of turtles, which evolved in Asia during the Cretaceous Period. They then spread across other continents, at one time extending into North America, while other members of the family occurred in Africa and Europe.

Whereas the actual shell scutes of this turtle are thin, the underlying bony layer is very strong. Indeed, the sutures become obliterated in older individuals, and the bone is thick, adding to the protective function of the shell. The scutes, in comparison, are easily worn away, especially if they come into contact with a rough surface, and damage to the underlying bone is then likely to occur. These turtles appear not to climb out of the water to bask on rocks, preferring instead to float at the surface. The presence of barnacles on their shells suggests that they may also venture into brackish waters.

Central American river turtles rarely emerge onto land, and so, not surprisingly, they are unable to walk effectively. This may well be a reflection of lack of muscular tone, however, as it appears that turtles, such as the red-eared slider (*Trachemys scripta elegans*), which are normally quite proficient on land, have difficulty in walking after being kept in a primarily aquatic enclosure for a period of time.

The lack of mobility of the Central American river turtle on land would inevitably prove a handicap during the breeding period. It has evolved a unique means of overcoming this difficulty, however, by nesting not during the dry season, when sandbanks would be exposed, but at the height of the rainy period, when the river is in flood. The turtles are then washed into narrow tributaries at the sides of the river and, barely leaving the water, they then bury their eggs just above the water-level. These are hard-shelled, and average about 20 in a typical clutch. As the waters recede, the eggs will develop without risk from further flooding.

The large size of these turtles makes them a popular target for local hunters throughout their range. Their white flesh is considered a delicacy in many parts and may have been responsible for the Mexican description of *tortuga blanca* (white turtle), which is applied to this species. Adults can grow to about 60 cm (2 ft) over all, and, once mature, they become essentially herbivorous in their feeding habits. River otters also prey on these turtles, probably preferring smaller individuals.

Family: Cheloniidae – Sea Turtles

Six out of the seven known species of sea turtle are included in this family, and range throughout the world's oceans, extending virtually to the tips of the southern continents and northwards almost to Scandinavia. The largest species is the loggerhead (*Caretta caretta*), and although those caught today seem relatively small, much bigger individuals have been recorded in the past. A skull originating from a loggerhead captured in Australian waters measures nearly 30 cm (1 ft) in diameter, and the turtle itself probably weighed as much as 540 kg (1,192 lb).

In contrast, the Atlantic or Kemp's ridley (*Lepidochelys kempi*) rarely exceeds 81 kg (180 lb), and its carapace measures about 75 cm (30 in) maximum. As its name suggests, this species is confined to the Atlantic, notably around the Gulf of Mexico. It is not uncommonly encountered on America's eastern seaboard, and may occasionally be seen off

Plate 55   The green turtle (*Chelonia mydas*) is undoubtedly the most economically significant of the marine turtles. Ranching of this species provides a potential means of meeting the demand for turtle products without harming the adult breeding population, as with the Hawksbill below.

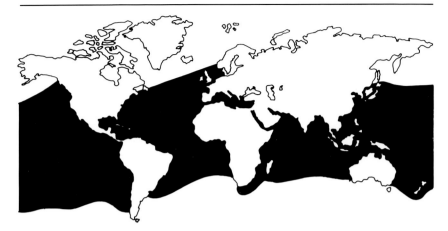

Map 4   Distribution of the family Cheloniidae.

European coasts. It may have become isolated after the closure of the Panamian land-bridge, about four million years ago.

The Olive ridley (*Lepidochelys olivacea*) is larger in size, and has a much wider distribution, extending into Pacific waters. Relatively little is known about the habits of this tropical species, in contrast to those of the equally wide-ranging green turtle (*Chelonia mydas*), which have been very extensively studied in various parts of its range. A number of interesting discoveries have been made as a result, including the fact that, in some areas in northern-central parts of the Gulf of California, the turtles actually become dormant when the temperature of the sea falls. They burrow into the sea bed, and remain here from about November through to March.

The size of the green turtle can vary quite considerably through its range. Those found on the beaches of Ascension Island and Surinam are the largest, with the record being held by a green turtle from the former locality, which measured 138 cm (55 in) across its carapace. This may be related in part to the lack of predation on the species when it nests on Ascension Island. Certainly, even bigger individuals occurred in the past, possibly weighing as much as 453 kg (1,000 lb). These were often found around the coast of Cedar Key, Florida, where today the species has become scarce, and only small individuals are recorded.

Where the turtles are hunted, there is little opportunity for individuals to grow to a large size. In spite of being highly prolific, and laying over 1,000 eggs in the course of a breeding season, green turtles are vulnerable to the effects of predators. Studies have shown that, in some cases, about one quarter of the population can be killed annually, while the turtles themselves only lay every three years on average. It is easy to see how a severe population decline can follow a sustained period of harvesting.

Controls on the exploitation of the green turtle, long favoured as the ingredient of turtle soup, have been increased during recent years. Nicaragua, for example, shut its processing plants during 1976, which may help to stabilise the decline of the neighbouring Tortuguero population in Costa Rica. Considerable effort has also been expended on establishing turtle farms, to ease the pressure on surviving wild turtles, in the hope that their numbers will increase again.

Attempts at farming have been compromised to some extent, however, by conservation controls established to protect the wild population, and administered internationally through agreement by the parties to the Convention on International Trade in Endangered Species of Fauna and Flora (CITES). The majority of sea turtles, with the exception of the flatback turtle (*Chelonia depressa*), are accorded Appendix I status under this agreement, preventing commercial trade in live animals, their parts or derivatives. There is a provision, however, for ranched populations to be listed in Appendix II, which permits trade under certain controls.

Amongst the various ranching schemes is a project being carried out on the French islands of Europa and Tromelin in the Indian Ocean. Studies began here on populations of the green turtle back in 1970 and, after a short break, have continued since 1977. Female turtles are tagged when they emerge for laying purposes, and the data obtained have confirmed that the turtles' reproductive cycle in the Indian Ocean is identical to that observed in the Caribbean, lasting about four years.

The number of hatchlings produced may vary quite considerably; on Europa for example, the estimated figure can range from 700,000 to 2.4 million, with some hatchlings emerging during the day. These may be used in the ranching enterprise. This island is ideally suited to being a breeding area for turtles, as access is restricted and it is only inhabited by military personnel and scientists. Similarly, Tromelin also offers protection to nesting turtles, and visitors are only permitted by agreement with the Reunion prefect responsible for the affairs of the island.

Problems have arisen over the rearing of the turtles taken as hatchlings to support the ranching operation, but these now appear to have been largely overcome. For example, the populations originally had a high incidence of skin disease, but, following research carried out at the University of Reunion, it is now clear that such disorders were of nutritional origin. Deficiencies of essential fatty acids were noted, and subsequent dietary modifications have led to a very significant reduction in mortality.

Criticism of ranching has also been mounted because of the high levels of fat present in the livers of turtles reared in confinement. Microscopic examinations have shown, however, that this is not pathogenic. Indeed, the turtle's liver normally acts as a labile fat depot, sustaining it on its often lengthy migration back to its nesting beach. By the time of arrival here, most of the fat stores have been exhausted, revealing a different histological picture.

There is no doubt, however, that captive-reared turtles grow at a much faster rate than their counterparts in the wild. They can weigh as much as 35 kg (77 lb) when only three years old, and this difference in growth rate also affects the shell, causing it to appear less convex. This

Plate 56 Education plays a key role in encouraging people to protect the wildlife in their area. This poster from Papua New Guinea is aimed at persuading the local people not to hunt turtles to extinction.

actually provides a means of distinguishing between wild-caught and ranched turtles, and would help to eliminate illegal trade. Similarly, the conspicuous absence of arachidonic acid from the tissues of ranched turtles provides a biochemical means of ascertaining their origins.

The green turtle is probably the most valuable chelonian in economic terms. It is a popular food, both traditionally in the areas where the species occurs, and further afield, as a gourmet's dish. Its shell is often a popular tourist souvenir when polished, and pieces are also used by furniture manufacturers. The scutes can be used in this way as a substitute for those of the hawksbill turtle (*Eretmochelys imbricata*), so that ranching of one species may help to conserve another.

One of the major problems in establishing ranching schemes of this type with endangered species, is to prevent adult wild turtles, which are so essential for maintaining the overall population, being drawn into the trade under the guise of being ranched themselves. Close supervision and marking systems are essential. Once such problems have been overcome, ranching may prove the salvation of this species and possibly others as well.

The high reproductive potential of sea turtles, and the correspondingly high level of mortality amongst hatchlings, means that a significant proportion of offspring can be removed at this early stage without any harmful effects on the overall population. It is usually preferable to work with hatchlings, as the transfer of eggs can lead to a significant decline, of perhaps 30 per cent, in their viability. An additional, but rarely stated benefit associated with ranching is the vast amount of scientific data accumulated on the species concerned. In this way, a better understanding of the requirements of wild populations can also be obtained.

Attempts to conserve Kemp's ridley have already been mentioned. These turtles, unlike the green turtles and other species with widely distributed nesting grounds, nest on just one stretch of beach in Mexico. The survival of the whole population is dependent on this tiny area. Unlike other turtles, Kemp's ridley is a diurnal nester, laying its eggs during the day in a much more rapid fashion than nocturnal egg-layers.

The turtles emerge from the surf as a group, forming the characteristic *arribada*, or 'arrival', with large numbers then laying communally on the beach. In 1947, when this spectacular event was first filmed, the population which came ashore was estimated to be 40,000, whereas within two decades it had fallen to just 5,000 in total. Unlike the mass beachings of the past, several smaller *arribadas* now take place. The turtles prefer to nest when there is a strong wind, as this helps to conceal their eggs after laying. Kemp's ridley is a relatively light turtle and does not leave a heavy track in the sand. When the wind blows, the sand on the beach above sea-level is quickly dispersed, concealing the excavations and the scent of the turtle's presence. It is thought that scent glands enable the *arribadas* to form in the first instance, and that the turtles may then congregate offshore until the weather conditions are favourable to disguise their transitory presence on the nesting beach, which is only about 20 km (12 miles) in length.

Reliable estimation of the numbers of this and other sea turtles is difficult, usually being based on the numbers of females emerging to breed. It seems unlikely that the overall population exceeds 5,000, and it could be less, making Kemp's ridley the most critically endangered of the marine chelonians. One strong point, which could be vital to its survival, however, especially if the American translocation project proves successful, is that females tend to have an annual breeding cycle, rather than an interval of several years between seasons. Clutches average around 110 eggs, and the adult turtle has usually completed her nesting activities within an hour of emerging onto the beach.

Much of the recent decline of Kemp's ridley stems from human activity, not only by direct predation on these turtles and their eggs, but from the activities of shrimp trawlers operating in the Gulf of Mexico. Unlike the green turtle, which feeds almost exclusively on marine vegetation when adult, this species favours crustaceans and similar creatures, and is thus readily drawn into shrimp nets. Here, they can become trapped and ultimately drown. It has been estimated that as many as 500 of these turtles used to be trapped in this way each year, but new requirements in trawling techniques have served to lessen this toll.

The hawksbill turtle (*Eretmochelys imbricata*) is another species which has suffered heavy human predation, although it is more widely distributed than Kemp's ridley. It is most commonly encountered around coral reefs and similar areas of shallow water, which leave it vulnerable to the spear-gun fishermen. Interestingly, these turtles feed on invertebrates, such as sponges, which often contain potent toxins. While these leave the turtle unaffected, occasional human deaths have resulted from consumption of these turtles, presumably because the toxins were still present in the animal's flesh.

Some hawksbills appear to be sedentary, rarely moving from one area, but others may undertake lengthy journeys across the oceans. Tagging records reveal that one such migrant travelled from the Torres Strait region of Australia, to nest on the beach at Kerehikapa in the Solomon Islands 11 months later, after a journey of about 3,600 km (2,237 miles). The nesting behaviour of this species tends to differ from that of other sea turtles, as nesting is rarely aggregated in any way. Many beaches are used, but often only one female will be found in the locality.

The scutes of this species are much in demand for ornamentation purposes, being known as tortoiseshell. This harvesting can be especially harmful for the species over all, as the largest individuals, which, in the case of females, are the most productive, are preferred for this purpose. It is very difficult to make an accurate assessment of population numbers, because of the hawksbill's nesting habits and its wide distribution. Attempts at ranching this species, with a view to supplying the market for tortoiseshell, especially in Japan where it has long been a traditional material for craft purposes, have not proved successful in the past. The advances being made with green turtles, however, may encourage more serious attempts with this species.

Young, stuffed hawksbills, rarely more than two years old, find a ready market as curios, in spite of international measures aimed at curtailing such trade. Already, in Indonesia, hatchlings are reared in captivity for this market, being killed at around six months of age, depending on their size. It is estimated that as many as 105,000 such turtles may be marketed each year through Indonesia, the Philippines and Singapore to avid tourists. Many of these are then confiscated on arrival back in Europe or elsewhere, as no permits have been obtained (and probably would not be issued in any event) to allow the import of this endangered species.

Family: Dermochelyidae – Leatherback Turtle

The leatherback (*Dermochelys coriacea*) is without doubt the most unusual of the marine turtles, not only in terms of its physical appearance, but also its distribution. It appears to have separated from the ancestral marine stock around 65 million years ago, and ranges much further out of tropical waters on a regular basis than other species. Several have been caught off the coast of Norway, and some have even been found in waters inside the Arctic Circle.

At the southernmost tip of its distribution, the leatherback may be encountered in the waters surrounding New Zealand, and close to the Chilean coast, as well as at the southern tip of Africa. Their ability to survive in these localities is highly indicative of at least partial endothermy, enabling these turtles to maintain a body temperature well in excess of their immediate environment.

The leatherback is the largest surviving marine turtle, and its size also probably conveys some degree of thermal insulation when it is in cold waters. Individuals weighing around 680 kg (1,500 lb) and measuring 1.8 m (6 ft) in carapace length are not unknown, but recent catches tend to suggest a maximum weight of about 453 kg (1,000 lb). Initial estimates of the leatherback's numbers, back in the early 1970s, are now seen as being very conservative. Other breeding grounds have since been discovered, and it appears that the overall population of the species is probably in excess of 100,000 individuals. Its future is more secure than that of members of the Cheloniidae, as it is not utilised to the same extent. Leatherbacks nest widely throughout tropical areas, but only a few large traditional nesting sites have been reported, and it is here that harvesting of the eggs represents the greatest danger to the population

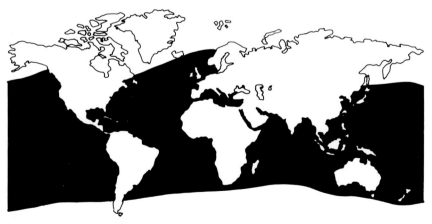

Map 5   Distribution of the family Dermochelyidae.

over all. Tourist development in such areas also poses a potential threat.

The leatherback is a turtle of the open sea, and appears to encounter difficulties in adapting to the confines of a pool, constantly attempting to swim through obstructions, such as a glass viewing area. The diet of this species also makes it difficult to keep, as it feeds almost exclusively on jellyfish and marine planktonic creatures such as sea squirts.

Its pelagic lifestyle also influences the leatherback's choice of nesting site. It avoids coral reefs, preferring instead to approach the beach directly from deep water, often through heavy surf. Once on land, nesting takes place quite rapidly, and the turtle returns to the water within a couple of hours. The leatherback tends to lay a relatively high proportion of malformed eggs, and this may be linked to the surprisingly short inter-nesting interval. Up to nine clutches may be laid in a season, with a gap of just ten days between each, and, on average, there are about 80 viable eggs in every clutch. The number of eggs laid differs somewhat according to the geographical area concerned, with the smallest clutches being produced in the eastern Pacific. The leatherback usually nests at mainland sites, rather than on small islands, and, although it is not well documented, the nesting interval seems to extend for several years.

Before leaving land, the leatherback circles its nesting site, as the hatchlings will also do in due course. This may facilitate their return to the sea, or reinforce the nesting site in their memory. There is no doubt that leatherbacks may undertake long journeys through the oceans. One individual, tagged at its nest site on a beach in Surinam, in northern South America, reappeared across the other side of the Atlantic, some 6,800 km (4,226 miles) away.

Family: Emydidae – Freshwater Turtles

The emydids are, certainly in numerical terms, the most successful family of chelonians at the present time. Allowing for classificatory arguments, approximately 136 species are recognised, with representatives of the family occurring on all continents apart from Australia. This large group is further subdivided into two sub-families, Emydinae and Batagurinae. They tend to be fairly homogeneous in terms of appearance, having moderately flattened shells, although the predominantly terrestrial species have a more highly domed carapace. Emydids usually have 24 marginal scutes around the carapace edge and a further dozen covering the plastron. Their coloration is extremely variable, and may show signs of patterning, as in the spotted turtle (*Clemmys guttata*), with orangey spots clearly apparent on its carapace. This is a North American species, like many other members of the family.

Not all are found in fresh water: the diamondback (*Malaclemys terrapin*) occurs in brackish areas. This species was almost brought to extinction in the early years of the present century, being relentlessly hunted for its flesh. In this regard, it suffered worse than the snapping turtles of the family Chelydridae, but it has since recovered in numbers.

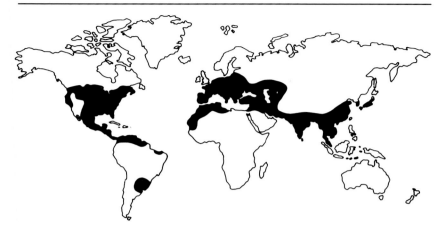

Map 6   Distribution of the family Emydidae.

Prohibition may have indirectly assisted its survival, as alcohol was an essential ingredient in the preparation of terrapin dishes for the table. During the period of peak demand, breeding farms were established for the species.

Diamondbacks show great variation in their markings. Seven sub-species are recognised, although, even within these groupings, differences are often apparent. The species is easy to sex, as males are smaller over all, both in terms of size and head shape, than females, averaging a carapace length of 12.5 cm (5 in) when mature.

These distinguishing features are apparent in members of the related genus *Graptemys*. These turtles are often known as sawbacks, because of

Plate 57   The Alabama map turtle (*Graptemys pulchra*) varies considerably in size, with females growing to nearly 30 cm (12 in) in length. Males, in contrast, rarely grow to a quarter of this size, and are also much quicker to mature, breeding when only three years old. Females may not nest until they are well into their teens.

Plate 58   The eastern painted turtle (*Chrysemys picta picta*) occurs in eastern North America, from Nova Scotia southwards to Alabama. It can be easily distinguished from other races because its costal and central scutes form a continuous line across the shell, rather than being disjointed.

the raised serrations running down the centre of their vertebral scutes. The rear marginals also frequently show a serrated pattern. *Graptemys* species are sometimes described as map turtles, because of the characteristic pattern of markings evident on their carapace and plastron. These, especially in young individuals, are said to resemble the contours of a map. Unlike many emydids, members of this genus tend to be highly aquatic, rarely walking far on land.

As a result, they have fairly localised distributions in a number of cases, depending on the extent of the water system in which they occur. The sexes have effectively evolved to occupy two distinct ecological niches within their range, reflected in part by their physical differences. Females, with their much more powerful jaws, feed largely on snails and fresh-water mussels, which they acquire in the main body of water. The smaller males, in contrast, as well as hatchlings, feed on various insects gathered in the shallows.

Another genus, which occurs exclusively in North America, is *Chrysemys*. There are four distinct sub-species of the painted turtle, described on the basis of their distribution. The nominate race is the eastern (*C. picta picta*), which, unlike other turtles occurring on the continent, has its vertebral and costal scutes running virtually parallel, so that the joins between them are effectively aligned. The carapace is dark in colour and, with the plain yellowish plastron, serves to distinguish this race. On occasions, these painted turtles can have a carapace length of just over 17.5 cm (7 in), but it is usually an inch or so less in most cases.

The midland painted turtle (*C. p. marginata*) overlaps through part of its range with the eastern, but is easy to distinguish, both by the overlapping pattern of scutes on the carapace and the dark markings confined to the centre of the otherwise clear plaston. In the case of the western race (*C. p. belli*), the carapace may show a series of yellowish streaks and the plastron tends to be mottled over the whole of its surface. This sub-species is the largest form, usually averaging 17.5 cm (7 in) when adult, and occasionally growing to nearly 25 cm (10 in). The southern race (*C. p. dorsalis*), is probably the easiest to recognise, as there is an unmistakable orange-red stripe running down the carapace from head to tail.

Painted turtles are surprisingly hardy and it is not unusual to see them swimming under ice during the winter. Both sexes are mature and ready to breed by about their sixth year. Males have long front claws, and stroke the female's face as a prelude to mating. If she responds, holding out the claws on her front feet to touch his feet, mating takes place. A typical clutch size varies from around three to as many as 11 eggs in older females.

The genus *Trachemys* is closely related to the painted turtle, but has a much wider distribution, occurring down through Central America as far south as parts of Uruguay and Argentina, where isolated populations of the black-bellied slider (*T. dorbignyi*) are found. The description 'slider', often applied to *Trachemys* species, would appear to stem from their habit of sliding back rapidly under water if they are disturbed while basking.

The best-known member of this genus is undoubtedly the red-eared

Plate 59   The red-eared slider (*Trachemys scripta elegans*) is well known, being widely kept as a pet in many parts of the world. Farming of this species is commonplace, both in its North American homeland and further afield in South-East Asia.

Plate 60   The western painted turtle (*Chrysemys picta belli*) is one of four distinctive sub-species. This is the largest race, sometimes growing to 25 cm (10 in). It is found in southern parts of Canada and the north-west United States, with populations as far south as Mexico.

slider (*T. scripta elegans*) which is reared commercially on turtle farms in the United States and Malaysia, for the pet market. Hatchlings are particularly attractive, characterised by the prominent red flashes present on both sides of the head. As with related turtles, their initial growth is fast, and they may reach 7.5 cm (3 in) by their second year. They then grow at about 1.25 cm (0.5 in) annually, attaining a maximum size of 20 cm (8 in) or so.

Trachemys scripta, of which at least a dozen sub-species are recognised, is widely distributed ranging from the south-eastern side of the United States into Central America. Representatives of this species also occur on various Caribbean islands, and in some parts of South America. They can be easily distinguished from related species by the shape of their mouths. Seen from the front, the lower jaw is curved, instead of being flat.

The nominate race, often described as the yellow-bellied turtle (*T. s. scripta*), may retain an uneven shell surface. This is believed to show the influence of the ancestral form, *Trachemys inflata*, which became extinct during the Pliocene Period, about seven million years ago. The shell of the yellow-bellied turtle is relatively thick, and this may offer some defence against alligators, which are often found in the same waters.

Other *Trachemys* species also inhabit the islands of the Caribbean, but they may be closely related to *T. scripta*. The species found on Puerto Rico, for example, known as *T. stejnegeri*, also has characteristic red markings behind its eyes, although its carapace is brownish rather than green, and has no markings on it.

Cooters, belonging to the species *Pseudemys concinna*, are more likely to be found in rivers and similar stretches of water, than lakes. The river

Plate 61 The markings of the red-eared slider, like those of related species, such as the cooter (*Pseudemys concinna*), vary widely. Older individuals tend to lose the markings on the carapace as they mature, and may darken in coloration.

cooter itself (*P. c. concinna*) may attain a carapace length of about 30 cm (12 in). Other sub-species, such as the mobile cooter (*P. c. mobilensis*), may grow slightly bigger. This particular turtle is often found close to the coast, inhabiting brackish waters. Cooters tend to become more vegetarian in their feeding habits as they get older. The large Suwannee cooter (*P. c. suwanniensis*), growing to around 40 cm (16 in), is said to feed exclusively on plants once it has matured.

The peninsula cooter (*Pseudemys floridana*) is found in south-eastern parts of the United States. Three sub-species are recognised, and over all, the species is characterised by its carapace, which has smooth edges, showing no trace of serrations. Its highest point is located between the centre of the shell and the head. These cooters can be relatively large, growing to nearly 40 cm (16 in), with the notable exception of the Missouri race (*P. f. hoyi*), which does not appear to exceed 30 cm (12 in).

The colourful appearance of many sliders is reflected by the various red-bellied turtles. The Plymouth red-bellied turtle (*P. rubriventris*) is one of the rarest North American chelonians. Its total population is believed to comprise around 200 individuals, half of which inhabit Federal Pond, in Carver County, while the others are concentrated in neighbouring Plymouth County. It has been calculated that the total annual output of these turtles is around 385 eggs, with about 100 hatchlings emerging each year.

In order to try to boost the numbers of this species, hormonal induction has been used to obtain eggs from gravid females. These are then incubated artificially, and the resulting young can be released back into the wild. By modifying the incubation temperature, increasing numbers of females can be produced, assisting the overall increase in population.

Similar techniques may need to be employed in the case of the Alabama red-bellied turtle (*Pseudemys alabamensis*), although this species is not yet so critically under threat. Its shallow nests, sometimes just 8 mm (3 in) below the surface, leave the eggs vulnerable to predators, such as fish crows (*Corvus ossifragus*), while alligators (*Alligator mississippiensis*) exert a heavy toll on immatures which do survive the hatching period.

A species which has been able to reduce its shell thickness by usually avoiding areas of water which could support alligators, is the chicken turtle (*Deirochelys reticularia*). It is found in small ponds and similar stretches of water, and, perhaps not surprisingly, proves quite mobile on land. This is not a large species, rarely growing beyond 17.5 cm (7 in), but proves an active hunter, well able to prey on creatures bigger than itself, such as crayfish. It has a relatively large mouth, and a highly distensible throat. The common name of the species is derived not from its feeding habits, but from the supposed taste of its flesh. The chicken turtle never attained the popularity of other turtles as a food dish, however, possibly because of its scattered distribution: it is generally not found in large numbers in any one locality.

A number of other members of the sub-family Emydinae are also

Plate 62   The chicken turtle (*Deirochelys reticularia*) inhabits shallow areas of water, such as ponds, rather than rivers and lakes. It is a North American species, ranging from Virginia to Texas.

semi-terrestrial in their habits. They include the four members of the genus *Clemmys*. The wood turtle (*C. insculpta*) is, in fact, found most commonly on land, and only remains submerged during the hibernation period. It is regarded as one of the most intelligent species and this has been confirmed by laboratory tests. The bog turtle (*C. muhlenbergii*), typically inhabiting marshy areas, does occasionally enter water to seek food. These turtles show a distinct preference for live foods such as invertebrates, but will also eat berries and greenstuff.

The most aquatic of the *Clemmys* species is the western pond turtle (*C. marmorata*), which, like other members of this group, appears to be becoming increasingly scarce in the wild. Habitat destruction, such as the draining of marshland, is an important factor in its decline. The highly terrestrial habits of the wood turtle also render it vulnerable to traffic during the course of its wanderings. These tend to be secretive turtles, however, especially when young, so they can be more numerous in an area than a casual visit might suggest.

Blanding's turtle (*Emydoidea blandingi*) has a relatively northerly distribution. It is also a semi-terrestrial species, but usually feeds in water. It is now considered most closely related to the chicken turtle (*Deirochelys reticularia*), although formerly it was grouped alongside the European

Plate 63   The European pond turtle (*Emys orbicularis*) varies considerably in appearance throughout its wide range, which extends from southern Europe into North Africa. It is found as far north as southern Poland, and grows to around 15 cm (6 in) in length.

pond turtle (*Emys orbicularis*) which it tends to resemble in appearance. The distribution of the European pond turtle actually extends into North Africa, and the northerly end of its range includes parts of Poland and Germany. Considerable variation in the patterning of this species is apparent. It used to occur in Britain, its fossilised remains having been discovered in East Anglia, dating back to 3000 BC, but the UK summers are now too cold to maintain a breeding population.

The other genus in the sub-family Emydinae has evolved into an almost totally terrestrial group. The box turtles forming the genus *Terrapene* have domed shells and are well protected from predators by their hinged plastrons. They are relatively small chelonians, rarely exceeding 15 cm (6 in) in size in the case of the eastern box turtle (*T. carolina*). Their coloration can vary widely, some individuals having bright markings, while others are predominantly brownish.

Plate 64   The eastern box turtle (*Terrapene carolina*) is most common in areas of woodland, where it feeds on invertebrates, berries and plants. These rank amongst the longest-lived chelonians, capable of surviving for a century or more. They rarely stray far from their home base.

Plate 65 The Mexican red turtle (*Rhinoclemmys pulcherrima*) is another
predominantly terrestrial species. Four sub-species are recognised: this one is
R. p. manni, which occurs in both Costa Rica and Nicaragua. It has a relatively
smooth carapace.

Box turtles are most commonly found close to wooded areas, foraging here for both invertebrates and fruit. They also eat plants on occasions. Mating occurs soon after the turtles emerge from hibernation, and a relatively small clutch of eggs, numbering from two to seven, will be laid later in the summer. Young box turtles lack an effective plastral hinge, and cannot, therefore, protect themselves like adults.

Six sub-species of *Terrapene carolina* are recognised, one of which, *T. c. triunguis*, is sometimes called the three-toed box turtle. The number of toes is not a reliable means of identification, however, especially as some members of this race may have four hind toes, and individuals belonging to other races also have three digits.

Whereas the eastern box turtle extends as far south as parts of Mexico, another member of this genus is confined to the central region of the United States. The ornate box turtle (*T. ornata*) overlaps through part of its range with the eastern, but hybridisation does not seem to take place. It tends to inhabit more arid areas, as does the localised species, *T. nelsoni*. The habits of this turtle are not well known, but it appears to be closely related to the ornate box turtle.

The final member of the genus is unique in that it is predominantly aquatic. The Coahuilan box turtle (*T. coahuila*) only occurs in a small area of Mexican marshland, feeding in shallow water. It is particularly vulnerable to any deterioration in its habitat, which is only 800 sq km (309 sq miles) in total.

The genus *Rhinoclemmys*, classified in the sub-family Batagurinae, appears to fill a similar evolutionary niche to the *Terrapene* species further south, with representatives ranging through Central America to South America and the Caribbean. Nine species are recognised, with those from the southern end of their distribution showing the typical tropical pattern of laying fewer, but larger eggs than their more northerly counterparts. Indeed, while the female herself can be only 20 cm (8 in) long, she may lay eggs with an individual length of 7.5 cm (3 in). Here, close to the Equator, there is no set nesting period, and so eggs can be laid at virtually any time of the year. The likelihood of the resulting hatchlings surviving is also increased, as they will be of a correspondingly larger size.

Some *Rhinoclemmys* species tend to be more aquatic than others. Whereas the Mexican form, *R. rubida*, is found entirely on land, the biggest species, found in Central America, is highly aquatic, as shown by its webbed feet. *R. funerea* can grow to over 30 cm (12 in) in size, and has a relatively flat carapace, presumably to assist its movements while in the water. *R. nasuta* is another aquatic member of the genus, from northern South America. It feeds on vegetation and fruit, being an agile swimmer inhabiting fast-flowing waters. When laying, as with some other species found in tropical areas, the female merely deposits the egg on the surface of the ground, and does not actually bury it. The position of the egg may be concealed by leaves, however, so that it is less vulnerable during the incubation period.

The majority of members of the sub-family Batagurinae tend to be

Plate 66 The snake-eating box turtle (*Cuora flavomarginata*) is another Asiatic species, not to be confused with the American box turtles of the genus *Terrapene*. The *Cuora* species are more aquatic by nature.

Plate 67 The Amboina box turtle (*Cuora amboinensis*) can seal itself totally within its shell, possessing hinged areas on its plastron for this purpose. It is semi-terrestrial in its habits, preferring to stay close to relatively shallow water.

from the Old World. There is often confusion between *Terrapene* box turtles, and those which are classified in this sub-family, belonging to the genus *Cuora*. These tend to be quite nervous turtles, and are more aquatic than their American counterparts. The hinged plastron in *Cuora* species is effective from hatching.

The Amboina box turtle (*C. amboinensis*) has the widest distribution of any of the four species, being found in relatively shallow areas of water, including paddy fields, through much of South-East Asia. At certain times of the year these turtles may spend longer periods on land, if observations on captive individuals form a reliable guide. Yellow head markings are common in members of this genus, whose distribution extends into China. They can grow to about 20 cm (8 in) in size, with shell coloration being darker in some individuals than others.

Often found in the company of *Cuora* species are the *Morenia* turtles, although virtually nothing has been recorded about their biology. When the water level falls during the dry season, the native people apparently catch these turtles for food.

A number of other emydids inhabit parts of South-East Asia, including the leaf turtle (*Cyclemys dentata*), so called because of its appearance. This is a predominantly aquatic species, in contrast to the other member

Plate 68   The leaf turtle (*Cyclemys dentata*) is clearly named because of its resemblence to a leaf. Mature specimens can be nearly 25 cm (10 in) in length, and only then do they develop a hinge at the front of the plastron.

Plate 69 The spiny turtle (*Heosemys spinosa*) is a native of South-East Asia, and can grow to about 20 cm (8 in). The function of the bizarre spines is unclear, although they may make it difficult for potential predators, such as snakes, to seize these turtles.

of the genus, *C. mouhoti*, which is primarily terrestrial, possessing a noticeably raised shell. The plastron develops a hinge in older specimens, and these turtles prove very adept at climbing, while their feet show some signs of webbing. It would appear similar in its habits to another Asiatic species, *Geoemyda spengleri*.

The genus *Geoemyda* has been extensively revised since its inception, and former members can now be found in the genera *Heosemys* and *Melanochelys*, amongst others. One of the most unusual species included in the former genus is the spiny turtle (*H. spinosa*), which has heavily serrated marginals. It has been suggested that they may protect these turtles from attacks by snakes. Four other species are now grouped alongside the spiny turtle, and all are said to be herbivorous, at least to some extent, in their feeding habits. In contrast, the related *Melanochelys trijuga* is probably omnivorous, in spite of some assertions to the contrary. These can grow to 37 cm (15 in) in size, about twice as large as the spiny turtle.

Plate 70   *Melanochelys trijuga* is a relatively dull-coloured chelonian, being predominantly brown or blackish in shell coloration. Six distinctive races can be identified, with individuals growing to around 25 cm (10 in) over all.

Plate 71   *Heosemys grandis* is a big species, as its name implies, reaching 42.5 cm (17 in) in size, but lacks the serrations which characterise the related spiny turtle (*H. spinosa*). When young, these turtles always have a soft area in the centre of the plastron.

Plate 72 Reeves' turtle (*Chinemys reevesi*) is a member of the large emydid group of predominantly fresh-water turtles. This is an Asiatic species, which appears to vary widely in size through its range. It does not often grow beyond 15 cm (6 in) in China, but individuals double this size have been recorded from Japan.

The Batagur (*Batagur baska*) is one member of this sub-family known to migrate during the breeding period, travelling a distance of perhaps 97 km (60 miles). Having excavated her nest, and then covered the eggs, the female turtle proceeds to disguise the area, by rising and falling on the sand, obliterating evidence of her digging activities. These rhythmic movements are said to resemble the sound '*tun tonk*', which has been corrupted to the name 'tuntong' for these turtles.

A related turtle, also found in parts of the Malay Peninsula, is *Callagur borneoensis*. This is probably the largest species of emydid, capable of attaining a carapace size of 75 cm (30 in). A slightly smaller species from the same area is *Orlitia borneensis*, growing to about 70 cm (28 in) in size. Other Asian turtles tend to be smaller, but one genus showing a wide variation in size among its seven species is *Kachuga*. Females are often larger than males and may be nearly 60 cm (24 in) over all in the case of the Burmese species *K. trivittata*, whereas the Indian roofed turtle (*K. tecta*) is barely one-third of this size.

Reeve's turtle (*Chinemys reevesi*) is one of the best known of the Asiatic emydids, and appears to grow larger in Japan than in other parts of its

Plate 73 The diamondback terrapin (*Malaclemys terrapin*) is one species which occurs in brackish water. It has a wide distribution along the American seaboard south from Massachusetts, and seven races are recognised. Individuals, even from the same area, differ quite widely in terms of their markings.

Plate 74 The snail-eating turtle (*Malayemys subtrijuga*) is found in slow-flowing stretches of water, and, as its name suggests, it feeds largely on snails. Mature individuals of this species can be 30 cm (12 in) in length.

Plate 75   The two-eyed turtle (*Sacalia bealei*) is characterised by at least one pair of yellow spots, complete with dark centres, resembling the pupils of eyes. Occurring in China, this species rarely exceeds 7.5 cm (5 in) in size.

range. The snail-eating turtle (*Malayemys subtrijuga*), from the Malay Peninsula, is quite often seen in captivity, and is easy to maintain in such surroundings.

The head camouflage patterning apparent in a number of sliders and related species is also seen in this sub-family. The species *Sacalia bealei*, for example, has at least two striking spots, resembling eyes, located directly on the top of the head. It is now realised that the supposed four-eyed turtle (*S. quadriocellata*) is also a member of this species. The number of spots may prove a means of distinguishing the sexes, with

Plate 76   The Caspian turtle (*Mauremys caspica*) has a wide distribution, from eastern Europe into parts of Asia and the Middle East, being found in Israel and Syria, as well as Crete and islands in the Aegean sea. Three sub-species are distinguished, both growing to around 20 cm (8 in) in size.

females tending to have four of these 'eyes'.

Apart from their distribution in Asia, this particular sub-family is also represented in Europe, by members of the genus *Mauremys*. These are relatively dull turtles in terms of coloration, with a dark carapace and striped markings on the head. Species range from Spain to North Africa, with the most easterly representative of the genus being *Mauremys japonica*, occurring in Japan.

The so-called Spanish turtle, now usually classified as a sub-species of the Caspian as *M. caspica leprosa*, is more common in the south of this country, extending across the Mediterranean Sea. In Africa, these particular turtles can be found as far south as Mali. Their shells are often badly infested with algae, and the description '*leprosa*' is said to stem from the appearance of this growth. The shell scutes may be raised, and the shedding of these, along with the algae, could be considered suggestive of leprosy, where external parts of the body are lost. Although fairly common in the past as pets, Spanish turtles are now rarely seen because of protective legislation enacted throughout much of their native range, especially in Europe. There is no evidence to suggest that the species is in decline.

Family: Kinosternidae – American Musk and Mud Turtles

This family comprises about 20 species, which are distributed from eastern parts of Canada down into South America. They are a fairly homogeneous grouping, characterised by a relatively large plastron, which is hinged but may lack the endoplastral component. Mud turtles (*Kinosteron* spp) can be distinguished on this basis, as their plastrons are hinged at both ends of the bridges, rather than just at the rear, as in the case of the musk turtles. They range in size from the large scorpion mud turtle (*Kinosternon scorpioides*), which may have a carapace length of just over 25 cm (10 in), to the flattened musk turtle (*Sternotherus minor*), unlikely to exceed 11 cm (4½ in).

The stinkpot turtle (*S. odoratus*) is one of the most widely distributed species, tending to prefer sluggish stretches of water. It ranges from southern Canada as far south as Texas, and possibly into Mexico, and is a relatively smaller species. Gaseous exchange probably takes place through the skin, enabling these turtles to remain submerged for long periods. They are highly aquatic by nature, and voracious carnivores, feeding on anything from carrion to crayfish.

In spite of their small size, this species, also known as the common musk turtle, has very powerful jaws, and can inflict a painful bite if handled carelessly. Males can easily be recognised, as they have characteristic rough pads on their hind legs, which assist in clasping the female during mating.

The scent of these turtles, which has given rise to their common name, is exuded whenever they feel threatened, and handling a wild individual will inevitably provoke this response. Once they are used to being picked up, however, stinkpots tend to lose this habit. These turtles appear to be quite social in the wild, with large numbers congregating in certain areas. It is not unusual for stinkpots to fall prey to fishermen, as they will often attempt to take bait off the end of a line. Females do come onto land when they lay, but rarely bother to excavate a nesting chamber.

Map 7   Distribution of the families Kinosternidae and Staurotypidae.

Plate 77   The loggerhead musk turtle (*Sternotherus minor*) is another primarily
aquatic species which can climb trees, and may bask off the ground on a branch.
Gaseous exchange in this species can occur through the skin when it is
submerged. When breeding, up to three eggs form the maximum clutch.

Instead, the eggs are concealed amongst vegetation, and may number up
to three in total.

Three species of musk turtle are recognised, with the race known as
Sternotherus minor depressus being the most distinctive. Occurring in a small
area of northern Alabama, it was not classified until 1955. Unlike other
members of the genus, which tend to have domed shells, the carapace of
this sub-species is flat and relatively wide. This may help these turtles to
remain hidden along the banks of the Black Warrior River where they
are found.

Plate 78 *Kinosternon abaxillare* has a localised distribution in the Mexican state of Chiapas. Growing in length to about 15 cm (6 in) over all, it is closely related to the scorpion mud turtle (*K. scorpioides*).

The mud turtles are a bigger group, comprising about 14 species. They lack the entoplastral bone of the plastron, which is unusual in chelonians. This seems to have occurred to enable development of the hinge at the front of the shell. Obviously, modification here is essential, altering the shape of this bone, which is usually diamond-shaped, to a triangular pattern, or else eliminating it from the plastron.

The degree of protection provided by the plastral hinges varies according to the species concerned. Some mud turtles, such as Herrara's mud turtle (*Kinosternon herrerai*), having a small plastron, are vulnerable in this regard. These all appear localised in their distribution, however, and may not be exposed to predators, so that a reduction in their body protection has taken place. Other species, such as the scorpion mud turtle, are able to retreat completely within their shells. One of the distinguishing features of this family is the presence of fleshy swellings, or barbels, around the neck. These probably have a respiratory function.

Several forms of the mud turtle are rare or endangered. The race known as the Illinois mud turtle (*K. flavescens spooneri*) is perhaps most threatened at present, although the centre of its limited area of distribution is now protected as a reserve. It may spend long periods, lasting up to nine months, including the winter, buried underground. For the remainder of the year, these turtles are primarily aquatic. Climatic changes several thousand years ago probably permitted this turtle to move into the arid terrain which it favours, but then its distribution became curtailed here as the climate altered again, and it now survives only in sandy areas with suitable stretches of water nearby.

144

Family: Staurotypidae – Mexican Musk Turtles

The three species in this family used to be classified with the Kinosternidae, as a separate sub-family, but they are now usually grouped apart. Inhabiting Central America, from Mexico to Honduras, these musk turtles are significantly larger than those occurring further north, growing up to about 38 cm (15 in). Throughout much of their range, these chelonians occur in waters alongside crocodilians, and their thickened shells offer increased protection against these reptiles. In addition, three prominent keels, which continue to develop with age, are also clearly apparent on the carapace, probably also for this reason. The head is broad and terminates in a pointed snout, with barbels present on the chin.

The guau (*Staurotypus triporcatus*) is a widely distributed species, and its large size makes it a popular target for local hunters. It appears to be highly predatory, as, in addition to feeding on molluscs, it also eats smaller *Kinosternon* species present in the same waters.

The Chiapas cross-breasted turtle (*S. salvinii*) tends to be slightly smaller, but coloration provides the best means of separating these two species. It has an orangish-yellow pattern of spots, contrasting with the white markings present on the head of the guau, and yellow rather than dark edges to its jaws. This turtle is said by local Indians to be able to eat its way out of a crocodile. Although this is unlikely, these turtles are certainly aggressive by nature.

The other member of the family is the narrow-bridged mud turtle (*Claudius angustatus*), which can be equally belligerent, especially when handled. Its long neck means that this chelonian can reach right round to bite on either side of the carapace. The narrow-bridged mud turtle shows a dramatic reduction in its plastral size, which may facilitate mobility. It probably occurs only in relatively shallow areas of water, out of reach of crocodiles. Indeed, it may aestivate after nesting during the onset of the dry period, when the waters dry up, by burying itself in the mud on the bottom of the pools where it normally lives. The Indians hunt these turtles at this time of year by prodding down into the mud with sticks. The distribution of this species appears to be centred in Mexico, although it also ranges into Belize and probably Guatemala as well.

Family: Testudinidae – Tortoises

Tortoises tend to occur mainly in tropical areas. Forty-one species are recognised, with representatives present on all inhabited continents apart from Australia. They are found in a variety of habitats, ranging from arid steppeland to tropical rainforests, and are primarily herbivorous, although fruit may predominate in the diet of forest species. Some tortoises will also take animal matter and invertebrates, even feeding on carrion in some cases. They range in size from the giant Aldabran species (*Geochelone gigantea*), with a carapace length of perhaps 140 cm

Plate 79 The red-footed tortoise (*Geochelone carbonaria*) varies somewhat in coloration throughout its wide range. Individuals which occur east of the Andes are relatively dark, with scarlet-red markings, whereas those found to the west tend to be paler over all, being more orange than scarlet.

(56 in), down to the small speckled tortoise (*Homopus signatus*) which is barely 210 cm (4 in) when fully grown.

The range of the family contracted following the end of the last Ice Age. In North America, changes from climatic alterations are most apparent, with species of the genus *Gopherus* now having a much smaller range than in the past. Three species still survive here, however, while a fourth is found in Mexico.

The desert tortoise (*G. agassizii*) extends as far north as southern California on the western coast of the United States. In areas where the winter temperature falls significantly, these tortoises burrow under-ground. They have powerful fore limbs for this purpose, and their tunnels may extend beneath the soil for a distance of at least 4½ m (15 ft), and sometimes considerably further. One gopher burrow is known to have been nearly 15 m (50 ft) in length. A number of other creatures are also found in these burrows, including the gopher frog (*Rana capito*), whereas more opportunistic species include various mammals, such as skunks and even burrowing owls. Rattlesnakes may also shelter within the tunnels of the gopher tortoises, and gassing, to drive out these reptiles, has proved harmful to the more sedate chelonian population in certain areas. Many invertebrates also live in close association with gophers: one study found over 32 such creatures in their burrows.

The gopher's need for suitable stretches of secluded land for tunnelling has led to its decline, as agricultural and urban development continue apace, eroding suitable areas of habitat. In semi-desert areas, the availability of food might appear problematical, but these tortoises are well able to eat thorny cacti, which contain a high level of water. They may also excavate hollows in the sand in order to establish a drinking area, while the interior of the burrow itself tends to be relatively humid, minimising water loss from the body while the reptile is underground. Gophers tend to follow a distinct set of paths from their burrows in search of food, and this exerts a natural control on the vegetation, encouraging the growth of particular grasses which the tortoises will crop at regular intervals. The tortoises also help to establish these plants

Plate 80   The yellow-footed tortoise (*Geochelone denticulata*) may sometimes be confused with its red-footed relative but, apart from coloration, these species can be distinguished on anatomical grounds. The gular scutes are divided in this species on the longitudinal axis, creating the appearance of four distinct scutes. In the case of the yellow-foot, the gulars do not reach the entoplastron, so that the interfemoral join is shorter than the interhumeral.

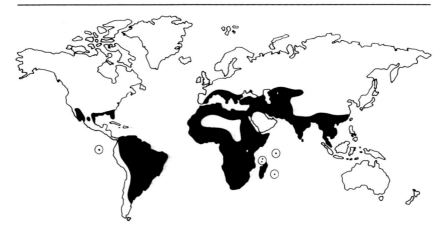

Map 8   Distribution of the family Testudinidae.

close to their burrows, as the seeds of the grasses are unaffected by the digestive process, and emerge in the faeces.

Gopher tortoises appear slow to mature, being unlikely to breed successfully until they are well over a decade old. They only lay relatively small clutches, numbering up to perhaps eight eggs, many of which fall victim to a range of predators. Research into the breeding habits of the Florida gopher (*G. polyphemus*) has revealed that nearly 90 per cent of clutches may be destroyed before the end of the incubation period, by creatures including striped skunks (*Mephitis mephitis*) and armadillos (*Dasypus novemcinctus*). The survival rate from egg-laying to the first anniversary of hatching is, realistically, less than six in 100. The most effective means of conserving this species is to protect its habitat, while attempting to exclude such predators, or transferring the eggs for artificial incubation.

Berlandier's tortoise (*G. berlandieri*) is found in southern areas of Texas, and ranges into north-east Mexico. This will also feed on cacti, notably *Opuntia*, when other food is in short supply. The other member of the genus is the Bolson tortoise (*G. flavomarginatus*), which was only discovered towards the end of the last century, and was first described as a separate species as recently as 1959. Its population is scattered, and upper estimates of numbers do not exceed 20,000 tortoises. This is a large species, with a carapace size which can approach 40 cm (16 in) over all, and it is now considered endangered. It used to range over a much wider area, extending north into Oklahoma, as fossil records have confirmed. It is not so surprising, therefore, that the Bolson tortoise more closely resembles the Florida gopher than the neighbouring Berlandier's tortoise, which is separated from the Bolson tortoise's present range by less than 160 km (100 miles). Today, the Bolson tortoise is confined to a tract of land barely 120 km (75 miles) long, and is still hunted in limited numbers by the local people. Captive-breeding schemes may yet play a vital part in preventing its extinction.

On the South American mainland, there are three surviving species of tortoise, two of which, the red-footed (*Geochelone carbonaria*) and the yellow-footed (*G. denticulata*) are closely related. They are found over a wide area of South America and their distributions overlap to some extent, although the yellow-footed does not occur west of the Andes, and is found further to the south west than the red-footed, in parts of Bolivia. It appears to be the larger species of the two, and can grow to a carapace size of 73 cm (29 in), although much over 50 cm (20 in) is unusual. The red-footed tortoise, in contrast, is not believed to exceed 45 cm (18 in), and averages around 30 cm (12 in) when adult.

These two species can also be distinguished on grounds of their appearance, with red-foots tending to be of brighter coloration over all, although individuals may vary quite dramatically in this regard. Those tortoises occurring west of the Andes (where the yellow-foot is not found)

Plate 81   The Galapagos giant tortoise (*Geochelone elephantopus*) is found on the islands located off the west coast of northern South America. Formerly heavily persecuted, some of the distinctive races became extinct, but the surviving colonies are protected. How their ancestors reached the islands, which arose in the middle of the ocean, is unclear. It is assumed that they drifted here from the mainland.

149

Plate 82   The Chilean tortoise (*Geochelone chilensis*) occurs in southern South America, and will retreat at night to a burrow to avoid the cold. In spite of its name, there is some doubt as to whether it actually occurs in Chile. It is also known as the Chaco tortoise.

tend to be paler, with orangish-yellow rather than scarlet markings on their extremities and shell, which is itself actually more brownish.

Both species are primarily forest-dwellers, feeding on fruits and vegetation, although, in some parts of their range, they are found in more open habitat. The reason for the occurrence of two such similar species in the same area is unclear. It has been suggested that the two forms diverged probably less than seven million years ago, from a common ancestor, described from its fossilised remains as *Geochelone hesterna*. This may have reflected differences in feeding habits, with one form preferring to browse on savannahs, whereas the other remained closely associated with a forest environment. Since then especially with human interference in the habitat of this part of the world, they would have tended to converge again. It is clear, however, that in spite of this overlap, both species exist independently, without hybridising. Observations suggest that males of each species can recognise each other by head movements, while cloacal scent differences enable interspecific matings to be avoided.

In view of their relatively large sizes, it is not surprising that these tortoises are hunted in many parts of their range. They are particularly in demand during Holy Week, the week before Easter, and can be seen then in many Indian markets, although there is no evidence to show any overall decline in the numbers of either of these tortoises. The red-footed, especially, is being bred in captivity. When mating, the smaller male utters a call rather like the clucking noise of a chicken, and around a dozen eggs form the usual clutch.

The other South American mainland species is the small and relatively dull Chilean or Chaco tortoise (*Geochelone chilensis*). In spite of its name, the centre of its distribution is actually Argentina. It is reported to occur in Chile, however, although this is not widely documented, and these tortoises may well have been introduced here from Argentina. Like the gophers (*Gopherus* spp), the Chaco tortoise typically excavates a shallow hole, or pallet, to which it can retire during the hottest part of the day, and at night. Deeper pallets are used during colder spells.

The status of the Chaco tortoise is unclear, as some taxonomists now recognise two distinct species, described as *G. donosobarrosi*, from northern Patagonia, and *G. petersi*, found in the central part of Argentina, although this latter form may simply be based on young specimens of *G. chilensis* itself. These tortoises are popular as a source of food, and may be declining in certain areas because of excessive collecting.

The Galapagos Islands, off the western coast of northern South America, are the home of one of the two surviving populations of giant tortoises. Since Charles Darwin first visited the islands and saw these huge chelonians on Chatham Island on 17 September 1835, many other naturalists have also visited to observe their habits. Unfortunately, earlier visitors to these islands were not as benign in their intentions. The Galapagos became a regular stopping point for ships, who replenished their meagre stores with giant tortoises. The unfortunate beasts could be kept alive on board without difficulty for long periods. Contemporary writers describe how these tortoises might survive for up to 14 months, without any sustenance, on vessels. They became popularly known as 'Galapagos mutton', although to some palates, probably jaded after months at sea, their flesh apparently tasted better than young pullets.

Twenty separate islands comprise the Galapagos group, and it was soon appreciated that different forms of tortoise could be found on these various islands. Unfortunately, some were exterminated before they were even known to scientists. The nominate population on Charles Island, christened *Geochelone elephantopus elephantopus*, was extinct by 1876, whereas the Barrington Island race disappeared even before it was described, about 1890. The ships had also brought other unwelcome visitors to the islands, which rapidly reduced the numbers of tortoises still further. Goats, which competed for the relatively sparse grazing, and rats, which preyed on the eggs and hatchling tortoises, were two animals introduced with devastating effects. There used to be at least 14 distinctive sub-species, which had evolved to suit the type of island where they occurred, although not all islands supported a giant tortoise colony.

The shell shape of the species has altered considerably in some cases, actually becoming raised above the neck, rather than being of the traditional domed shape. Sub-species with raised carapaces of this type belong to the saddle-backed group, and tend to be found on the more arid islands, where vegetation is less readily available. As they were not seriously threatened by predators in their isolation, the raising of the shell did not present any threat to the tortoises' survival, yet it enabled them to raise their heads higher. This meant that they could browse on taller vegetation, such as shrubs, which would be less likely to suffer from drought than plants growing on the surface of the land, having a deeper root system.

In turn, it appears that plants, such as the prickly pear cactus (*Opuntia*), which would be vulnerable to the browsing habits of the saddleback giants, have also become modified. On islands such as Abingdon, they have tended to adopt a tree-like manner of growth, evolving a layer of bark, so that the fleshy pads of the cactus are kept largely out of reach of the tortoises. This modification is not seen on islands where tortoises are absent.

On Volcan Wolf, however, both saddle-backed and domed tortoises occur together. This volcanic region on the largest island, called Albemarle, may have become modified during the recent geological past, so that the two races have come into close contact with each other. On this particular island, several distinctive sub-species, associated with various volcanoes, can be found.

While some populations of the Galapagos tortoise still survive, and have increased in numbers due to more enlightened conservation policies, the legacy of past, irreparable damage is still apparent. The tortoises on Abingdon were especially vulnerable, because this island was the first to be encountered by whaling ships tracking south. The sub-species here (*G. e. abingdoni*) could attain a carapace size of 100 cm (40 in) and possessed a thin shell. It did manage to survive the onslaught of the whalers, but the illegal introduction of just three goats to the island, in 1959, spelt its demise. One single male was discovered during 1971, and this was transferred to the care of the Darwin Research Station in the following year. Sadly, it appears that this male is destined to die alone, the last living example of the race. Further surveys have failed to locate any trace of other tortoises surviving on this island.

A similar fate befell the populations of giant tortoises occurring on the other side of the world, on the Mascarenes and Seychelles. While four of the Galapagos races are now extinct, and five are clearly still threatened, other tortoises in the Indian Ocean suffered even more because of human predation. By the beginning of the nineteenth century, three out of the four races had already vanished, leaving only the Aldabran giant tortoise alive here today.

Plate 83   The Aldabran giant tortoise (*Geochelone gigantea*) is the only surviving giant species in this part of the world, although formerly they were much more widely distributed here, with populations being established on Mauritius, the Seychelles and other neighbouring islands.

Our knowledge of the extinct populations is even less well documented than in the case of the Galapagos tortoises. Certainly, they were numerous on the island of Rodriguez, where thousands of individuals could be found. It appears that, here again, a saddle-backed form (classified as *Geochelone vosmaeri*) could be found, alongside a smaller, domed-shelled species, christened *G. peltastes*. These two groups appear not to have competed with each other, but fed in different vegetative strata, with *G. vosmaeri* browsing rather than grazing. *G. vosmaeri* could apparently weigh up to 45 kg (100 lb).

As the tortoises declined in numbers, so ineffective attempts were made to curb trade, but it continued with as many as 10,000 tortoises being transported annually from Rodriguez alone. Some of these were destined to be translocated to Mauritius, where the two native species were already well into decline. The original stock was extinct by 1760, and the last tortoises seen on Rodriguez vanished just 35 years later.

Aldabra remained largely untouched as a colony until 1889, when more responsible attitudes to the destruction of wildlife were becoming apparent. This undoubtedly safeguarded the population here. The

Plate 84   A close-up view of the characteristic spurs of the African spurred tortoise (*Geochelone sulcata*). This is a large species, occurring in a band across most of the continent south of the Sahara. It also retreats to a burrow, or pallet, but in this case, it is often to escape the sun's heat when it is at its fiercest, rather than the cold.

Plate 85   The carapace of a mature spurred tortoise may measure in excess of 60 cm (24 in), with males tending to be significantly larger than females. Mating appears only to take place during the wet season.

Aldabran giant tortoise (*Geochelone gigantea*) is now considered in no danger of extinction, and the total population of this species may be as many as 100,000 individuals. Small populations have been moved to various neighbouring islands, such as the Seychelles, where a breeding colony was set up at the end of the last century, to ensure that the species would have an increased chance of survival as Aldabra took in more settlers. Certainly some decline in its numbers may have taken place during the latter part of the nineteenth century, but it was nowhere as great as that which occurred on other Indian Ocean islands.

These tortoises often wallow in mud, and this seems to afford a means of protection against the myriad mosquitoes found on Aldabra. By coating the fleshy parts of its body with mud, the tortoise creates a protective layer which may act as a deterrent to the probing proboscis of the mosquito.

The tortoises found on mainland Africa today are significantly smaller than these island giants. The biggest species is the spurred tortoise (*G. sulcata*), which may attain a size of 75 cm (30 in). It is found in very arid areas, where there is often no surface water for many years, and, typically, buries itself in a pallet during the hottest weather. This is rarely much bigger than the tortoise itself. Its prominent femoral spurs appear to have no real functional significance, although the skin of this tortoise is considerably thickened, presumably to restrict water loss.

155

Whereas the spurred tortoise tends to be confined to northern parts of Africa, bordering on the Sahara Desert, from Senegal across to the Red Sea, the leopard tortoise (*Geochelone pardalis*) is more widely distributed over southern areas, extending northwards to the Sudan and Ethiopia. Individuals from South Africa tend to be larger than those occurring elsewhere, growing to 65 cm (26 in) in size. Leopard tortoises have a colourful pattern, most apparent on their carapace, although there is considerable variation in this regard. They are found in a wide range of habitats, as their distribution suggests, and are well able to survive in areas of fairly arid grassland.

Another colourful African *Geochelone* species is the radiated tortoise (*Geochelone radiata*), which is confined to the island of Madagascar (Malagasy). Here, its natural area of distribution covers an area of just 19,680 sq. km (7,600 sq miles). Unfortunately, although not traditionally persecuted by the local Antandroy people, this species has become valued for aphrodisiac reasons by Chinese settlers. This fact, coupled with alterations to the vegetative cover of the region, most notably the decline of the spiny cactus, *Opuntia*, which used to provide a refuge for these tortoises, has caused concern for their survival. Captive breeding is possible, however, so the numbers of the species can be increased by this means. One of the smallest tortoises, *Pyxis arachnoides*, has a similar attractive pattern of markings, said to resemble the appearance of a spider's web. Both this species and *P. Planicauda* occur on the island.

The other endemic tortoise on Madagascar is the angonoka (*Geochelone ynipkora*), which is in an even graver situation than the radiated tortoise. It has a pronounced domed carapace, and a significantly enlarged gular prong, which tends to curl in an upward direction. This tortoise may well be the rarest surviving species, living in an area of just 100 sq km (39 sq miles), although the precise reasons for its scarcity are unclear. Some suggest that it has become too specialised, its gular prong actively interfering with its feeding habits. In the recent past, however, it used to be more numerous, and was regularly exported as food by Arab traders visiting Madagascar, who shipped the animals to the nearby Comoro Islands. Locally, the natives consider this tortoise taboo as a food source, being known as a *fady*. Apart from conservation of its habitat, the future of the angonoka in the wild would appear to rest heavily on the control of feral pigs which dramatically reduce its breeding potential. Observations on captive tortoises of this species have revealed that the gular prong is used during mating, the male positioning it close to the female's leg, encouraging her to alter the position of her shell.

Africa has more species of tortoise than any other continent, although not all of these are large in size. The southern part of the continent is inhabited by some of the smallest tortoises, notably members of the genera *Homopus* and *Psammobates*. These tend to be colourful species. The African serrated tortoise (*P. oculifer*) also has a much serrated edge around its carapace, with the marginal scutes being modified.

The serrated appearance of the marginals is also seen in two of the hingeback (*Kinixys*) species. Home's hingeback (*K. homeana*) can be dis-

Plate 86   The Mediterranean spur-thighed tortoise (*Testudo graeca*) may appear
superficially similar to Hermann's (*T. hermanni*), but in terms of its shell
structure, it does not have a divided supracaudal scute. In addition, it tends to
grow to a larger size, measuring as much as 30 cm (12 in) or so.

Plate 87 The eroded or rosy hingeback (*Kinixys erosa*) tends to be a reddish-brown colour over all. It is characterised by the smooth slope over the rear of its carapace, which distinguishes it clearly from Home's hingeback (*K. homeana*). Large specimens can be just over 30 cm (12 in) in length.

tinguished from the eroded hingeback (*K. erosa*), however, by a pronounced vertical drop at the end of the carapace, whereas the shell profile of *K. erosa* is rounded. The latter tends to be reddish in coloration, whereas Home's hingeback is often a dark shade of brown. The most dramatic variations in coloration, in the case of this genus, are apparent in Bell's hinge-back (*K. belliana*), which ranges widely over central and southern parts of the continent. Some individuals may only have a brown carapace, whereas others will show a patterned shell, with markings not unlike those of the leopard tortoise. This particular species is more commonly observed in open savannah, unlike the other two hinge-backs. Another East African species, the pancake tortoise, found in rocky areas of Kenya and Tanzania, hides itself away under stones, well protected by its flattened body shape.

The genus *Testudo* is also represented in Africa, by the Mediterranean spur-thighed tortoise (*T. graeca*), which used to be commonly imported into Britain and other European countries as a pet, before this trade was made illegal under European Community legislation. Its distribution extends to the Middle East, and here tortoises are vulnerable to aerial predators. Both golden eagles (*Aquila chrysaetos*) and bearded vultures (*Gypaetus*) are known to prey on these reptiles. Adult tortoises, which can grow up to 25 cm (10 in), are seized from the ground and then released once the birds are about 30 m (82 ft) or so up in the air. It usually takes several drops to split open the shell, enabling the bird to feed on the tortoise's vulnerable body, and, on one occasion, eight such falls were necessary. The rate of predation can be quite high, especially when the birds of prey have chicks in the nest. A single pair accounted for no less than 84 tortoises in this fashion over a four-month period.

Since the ban on trade in *T. graeca* and Hermann's tortoise (*T. hermanni*), increasing concern has been voiced about the attitudes of the people

Plate 88   Hermann's tortoise (*Testudo hermanni*) was one of the species commonly available as a pet in northern Europe, until this trade was banned. Unlike the other species concerned, the Mediterranean spur-thighed (*T. graeca*), Hermann's lacks the spurs located close to the top of the hindlegs, and also has a longer tail which ends in a spur.

Plate 89   The Greek or marginated tortoise (*Testudo marginata*) can be easily distinguished from other *Testudo* species by its flared posterior marginals, although this feature may be less obvious in young individuals. It is confined to southern parts of Greece.

in areas where these tortoises used to be collected as pets. Now that they are considered essentially worthless, they are apparently being destroyed by barbaric means in certain localities. In some places pits are dug, partially filled with living tortoises which are then ignited with petrol, while others meet an equally unpleasant end as living hardcore for road-building operations. In Greece, the flesh of the marginated tortoise (*Testudo marginata*) has been used as a substitute for green turtle meat in some processing plants. *Testudo* species are also being used as animal food in some areas, but are rarely popular in their own right as a food source in Europe. A possible exception is Horsfield's tortoise, formerly grouped in the *Testudo* genus, but now more commonly described as *Agrionemys horsfieldi*. These chelonians have been caught and even exported as food from Kazakhstan for many years, around 150,000 being caught each year.

While European tortoises tend to be quite small, the *Geochelone* species found in Asia are significantly bigger, although nowhere near as large as those which formerly used to occur in this part of the world. The largest likely to be encountered today is the Burmese brown tortoise (*Geochelone emys*), with a carapace length of at least 45 cm (18 in) when mature. As a result of the heavy prominent scales on the thighs, this species is also known as the six-footed tortoise. It occurs in upland areas, often alongside the scarcer impressed tortoise (*G. impressa*), which tends to vary in coloration. Some individuals are much darker than others.

Plate 90   The Burmese brown tortoise (*Geochelone emys*) is the only species of chelonian, as far as is known, which shows any degree of maternal protection towards its eggs, remaining close to the nest site for a few days after laying.

Plate 91 The yellow tortoise (*Geochelone elongata*) is also known as the elongated tortoise, because of its relatively long, narrow shape. It tends to be nocturnal in its habits and feeds largely on fruit in the wild.

The elongated tortoise (*G. elongata*) has a relatively narrow carapace, which is yellowish-brown, augmented with black markings. It can grow to a size similar to *G. impressa*, attaining a shell length of about 27.5 cm (11 in). A closely related species from the same region is the Travancore tortoise (*G. travancorica*). Similar means of recognition to those described for the two predominantly South American species, *G. carbonaria* and *denticulata*, appear to prevent hybridisation between these two similar species. The apparently related island species known as the Celebes tortoise (*G. forsteni*) may, in fact, be simply an introduced population of

Plate 92   The starred tortoise (*Geochelone elegans*) is one of the most attractive species of chelonian. Although striking when seen in isolation, this patterning provides very effective camouflage in dry grassland.

the Travancore tortoise, which is established here and on Halmahera, Indonesia.

Links with African *Geochelone* species are clearly seen in the case of the star tortoise (*G. elegans*), which, with its characteristic radiated pattern of markings, is found on off-shore islands including Sri Lanka, as well as on the Indian sub-continent. Males tend to be much smaller than females, which themselves are unlikely to exceed 25 cm (10 in). A rarer form of starred tortoise, known as the Burmese (*G. platynota*), occurs largely in Burma as its name suggests. It is apparently a popular food item here, but virtually nothing has been documented about this species.

Family: Trionychidae – Soft-shell Turtles

Map 9   Distribution of the family Trionychidae.

This widely distributed family comprises 22 species, occurring in both temperate and tropical areas of the world. No members are found in either Central or South America or Australia, but elsewhere they can be found in a range of habitats. They are highly aquatic and well adapted to survive for long periods underwater, respiring via both skin and pharynx while submerged.

The actual shape of the 'shell' tends to vary, although it is usually flattened. In the case of the sub-family Cyclanorbinae, the shell elements tend to be less reduced, while skin flaps help to protect the rear feet. African members of this group rank amongst the biggest of the fresh-water turtles. The Senegal soft-shell (*Cyclanorbis senegalensis*), for example, can grow to a size of about 60 cm (2 ft), but whether the skin flaps are of any real value in deterring a predator is open to doubt. The Indian spotted turtle (*Lissemys punctata*) is smaller, rarely exceeding 25 cm (10 in) and, unlike some other species, it may be found in fast-flowing rivers. Study of its skeletal structure reveals bony elements which appear analogous to the peripheral bones found in members of other families, and the carapace itself is covered in yellowish dots. Females tend to grow to a significantly larger size than males.

In America, the Florida soft-shell (*Trionyx ferox*) grows to the greatest length, with females being as large as 50 cm (20 in). This species occurs alongside the spiny soft-shell (*T. spinifer*) in some areas. Like other related species, these are aggressive predators, feeding on a wide variety of water creatures. The spiny soft-shell is characterised by having projections protruding from its carapace, of variable length, depending on the sub-species concerned. Coloration differences between the sexes may be apparent, with males retaining the appearance of juveniles even when adult, having a series of black dots or 'ocelli' present over their carapaces. In fast-flowing stretches of water in the central part of the United

States, the smooth soft-shell (*T. muticus*) is more likely to be encountered.

The giant of the genus, which has also apparently adapted to a marine existence off the coast of Turkey, is the Nile soft-shell (*T. trionguis*). It is the only member of the genus present in Africa, and can grow to 90 cm (3 ft). The yellow spots seen in immatures tend to be lost in older individuals. The Indian *Trionyx* species are the most attractive in terms of their coloration, such as the peacock soft-shell (*T. hurum*), but again the markings fade as the youngsters get older.

The patterning on the carapace of the narrow-headed soft-shell undergoes a similar alteration. This species, classified separately as *Chitra indica*, is said to grow to as much as 90 cm (6 ft), and may even attack goats, overturning them. Another large species is *Pelochelys bibroni*, which is relatively common in southern Asia, extending into China, and also present on the Philippines. The record size in this instance is said to be 127.5 cm (51 in).

Plate 93   The Malayan soft-shell (*Trionyx subplanus*) has a leathery shell, like other soft-shells. They are predominantly aquatic in their habits and, deprived of the protection of a thick shell, tend to be highly aggressive by nature.

165

Family: Platysternidae – Big-headed Turtle

Map 10   Distribution of the family Platysternidae.

The sole member of this family is found in Asia, inhabiting mountain streams. It is thus used to relatively cold surroundings. Its common name stems from the size of its head, which can be half as wide as the carapace. The head is too big to be retracted under the shell, and so, for added protection, the species has a bony roof, with a tough outer scute on top of the head, extending down the sides of the face. The big-headed turtle can inflict a painful bite with its powerful jaws. They are skilful climbers, and may feed out of the water, although little is known about their habits in the wild. Two eggs appear to form the usual clutch, and the young hatchlings are said to be able to squeak if directly threatened, by being handled, for example. Their long muscular tails also assist in climbing, and they may sometimes be found in trees, according to some reports.

Sub-order: Pleurodira – Side-necked Turtles

Family: Chelidae – Snake-necked Turtles

This group of side-necked turtles is confined to parts of eastern South America and Australia, with the family also occurring on New Guinea. In evolutionary terms, they tend to be considered more advanced than members of the other family, Pelomedusidae, showing more specialisation in the area of the skull, for example.

A number of species have exceptionally long necks, and a characteristic feature of the family is the presence of convex articulations at both ends of the fifth and eighth cervical vertebrae. The neck can be almost as long as the shell in some cases, notably in members of the Australian genus *Chelodina*, which includes the giant snake-necked turtle, with a shell size of up to 30 cm (12 in), and the South American *Hydromedusa* species. Another rare feature of the *Chelodina* turtles is the high incidence of scute variation affecting the carapace. They often have six or more

Plate 94   The big-headed turtle (*Platysternon megacephalum*) is one of the most distinctive chelonians, with its large head which cannot be fully retracted back into the shell. Note the tongue clearly shown in this photograph.

vertebral scutes, in contrast to the established pattern of five associated with members of this sub-order.

The best-known turtle in the family is almost certainly the mata mata (*Chelus fimbriatus*), found in parts of the Amazon River, and in Trinidad. It has a long snout, somewhat reminiscent of a soft-shell turtle, which is used as a snorkel in a similar way when the turtle is in shallow water. Its carapace helps this species to blend in with its surroundings, and while

167

Map 11   Distribution of the family Chelidae.

Plate 95   The Spix's snake-necked turtle (*Platemys spixii*) is found in eastern Brazil and northern parts of Argentina. It can be distinguished from the species (*P. radiolata*) Brazilian by its dark plastron.

168

Plate 96   The toad-headed turtle (*Phrynops hilarii*) can grow to nearly 45 cm
(18 in). Note the pronounced chin barbels in this species, which occurs in
southern parts of Brazil as well as northern Argentina and Uruguay.

the limbs are poorly developed, the mata mata has a very powerful neck.

Instead of actively pursuing prey, it tends to lure fish within striking
distance, relying on its powerful neck to seize the prey. Rather than
adopting an angling technique, like the alligator snapping turtle (*Macroclemys temmincki*), the mata mata actually trawls the water, making
lateral movements with its flattened head to grab its objective. Interestingly, the eyes in this species are very small, which tends to indicate
they are of little value in its technique of capturing prey. Instead, it
seems that the mata mata, unlike most chelonians, relies on auditory
stimuli for this purpose. The tympana on both sides of the head can
detect water vibrations, thus providing an accurate indication of the
prey's position. The jaws of the mata mata are not powerful, and rather
than seizing prey by this means, it is simply sucked into the body, using
the well-developed hyoid apparatus in the throat. Other sensory input is
derived from the fleshy folds around the head.

The mata mata is probably most closely related to the *Hydromedusa* species, but whereas these turtles have continued to rely on their sense of vision, inhabiting relatively clear water, the mata mata needed to develop different mechanisms to find prey in murky surroundings.

In view of the distribution of the family today, it seems likely that the present-day continent of Antarctica was involved in its spread, even if this is not the ancestral home of this group of turtles. Other side-necks found in South American waters include the common toad-headed turtle (*Phrynops nasutus*), which has characteristic sensory barbels on its chin, and the three species in the genus *Platemys*, of which *P. platycephala* is best known, being described as the twist-neck turtle.

Family: Pelomedusidae – Afro-American Side-necks

Part of the South American distribution of this family overlaps with that of the Chelidae, with other representatives being found on mainland Africa and offshore islands, including Madagascar. The mesoplastral component is present in the shell in this instance, and there is no trace of a cervical scute.

One of the largest members of the group, and also of commercial significance, is the Arrau River turtle (*Podocnemis expansa*). It is not unknown for females of this species to grow to about 87.5 cm (35 in) in terms of shell length, and they can weigh upwards of 90.6 kg (200 lb). The species has a very wide range throughout the waterways of South America, but has become vulnerable because of its habit of nesting during the dry period, with large numbers of females congregating at suitable sites. Another factor, reminiscent of the behaviour of sea turtles, is the discovery that females will not lay every year, but appear to cycle about every four years.

The sheer scale of exploitation has created problems with regard to this species. It lays large clutches, often comprising more than 100 eggs, but now the sandbanks where the females come ashore are populated by

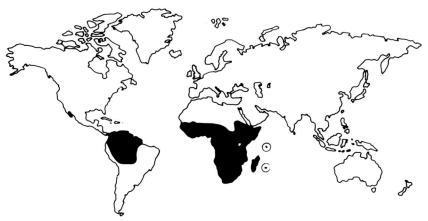

Map 12   Distribution of the family Pelomedusidae.

Plate 97   The black African mud turtle (*Pelusios niger*) occurs in West Africa, and may measure nearly 22.5 cm (9 in) in overall length. Other members of this genus are also found in the area south of the Sahara, although the precise number of species is a matter of taxonomic opinion, varying between five and eleven.

far fewer individuals than in years gone by. On the Orinoco beach in Venezuela, for example, the numbers have fallen on a staggering scale. In 1945, about 123,600 Arrau River turtles nested here, but by 1969, the total had fallen progressively to just 13,800. Now protection of the nesting sites is beginning to yield dividends in some areas, and the numbers of these turtles are slowly beginning to increase again. Movement of limited numbers of hatchlings to new areas has also proved effective. The other *Podocnemis* species are not persecuted to the same extent as *P. expansa*, although they can grow to well over 30 cm (12 in). The side-neck *P. unifilis*, for example, occurs in much the same area, but inhabits lakes and other still stretches of water.

The other major genus in this sub-family is the African mud turtle (*Pelusios* spp). These are found over much of the continent, south of the Sahara, although the precise number of species remains contentious. These African mud turtles are not especially colourful chelonians, and are of medium size, growing to about 30 cm (12 in) over all. Sensory barbels may be present on the chins of some species.

The Central African mud turtle (*P. castaneus*) now ranges outside Africa, occurring on the French West Indian islands of Marie Galante

Plate 98 The helmeted turtle (*Pelomedusa subrufa*) is similar to the *Pelusios* species, although there is no hinge on its plastron. It has a wide distribution, being found even in Madagascar. It often lives in temporary areas of water, moving from one pool to another as they dry up, then aestivating when no other option is available.

and Guadeloupe. It is possible that these turtles were carried across the Atlantic by the North Equatorial current, as there is no record of them being deliberately introduced at these localities. These turtles could be descended from the West African race *P. c. derbianus*, or they could have come from further south, their ancestors being picked up instead by the warm Caribbean current, which passes directly into their region.

The helmeted turtle (*Pelomedusa subrufa*) is another widely distributed side-neck, found in similar areas to *Pelusios* species. It differs in the lack of a plastral hinge and variations to the structure of the mesoplastral shell components. Its shell is quite thin overall, and this loss of weight may assist the mobility of this species on land. Helmeted turtles will frequently move from one area of water to another as their shallow pools dry up, or, alternatively, may aestivate in the mud at the bottom until the rains return. The species appears to have a relatively high reproductive capacity, laying over 40 eggs in a single clutch.

The adaptability of the chelonians as a family is readily apparent from the length of time that the group has been represented on this planet, and some species will almost certainly continue to expand their range in the future. The versatility and high reproductive potential of many species should ensure their continued survival, assuming that human interference does not destroy breeding populations. Otherwise, the sad consequences of the uncontrolled harvesting of the giant tortoises from the Galapagos and Indian Ocean islands will once again become apparent, adding to the list of extinctions caused by human intervention.

Appendix: Tortoises and Turtles of the World

Cryptodires: Sub-order Cryptodira

Fly River turtle: family Carettochelyidae

New Guinea plateless turtle *Carettochelys insculpta*

Sea turtles: family Cheloniidae

Loggerhead turtle *Caretta caretta*
Flatback turtle *Chelonia depressa*
Green turtle *Chelonia mydas mydas*
                  Chelonia mydas agassizi
Hawksbill turtle *Eretmochelys imbricata imbricata*
                  Eretmochelys imbricata bissa
Kemp's ridley *Lepidochelys kempi*
Olive ridley *Lepidochelys olivacea*

Snapping turtles: family Chelydridae

Common snapping turtle *Chelydra serpentina serpentina*
                  Chelydra serpentina acutirostris
                  Chelydra serpentina osceola
                  Chelydra serpentina rossignoni
Alligator snapping turtle *Macroclemys temmincki*

Central American river turtle: family Dermatemydidae

Central American river turtle *Dermatemys mawi*

Leatherback turtle: family Dermochelyidae

Leatherback turtle *Dermochelys coriacea*

Emydid turtles: family Emydidae

Subfamily Emydinae

Painted turtle *Chrysemys picta picta*
                     Chrysemys picta belli
                     Chrysemys picta dorsalis
                     Chrysemys picta marginata
Spotted turtle *Clemmys guttata*
Wood turtle *Clemmys insculpta*
Pacific pond turtle *Clemmys marmorata marmorata*
                     Clemmys marmorata pallida
Bog turtle *Clemmys muhlenbergii*
Chicken turtle *Deirochelys reticularia reticularia*
                     Deirochelys reticularia chrysea
                     Deirochelys reticularia miaria
Blanding's turtle *Emydoidea blandingi*
European pond turtle *Emys orbicularis*
Barbour's map turtle *Graptemys barbouri*
Cagle's map turtle *Graptemys caglei*
Yellow-blotched map turtle *Graptemys flavimaculata*
Common map turtle *Graptemys geographica*
Black-knobbed map turtle *Graptemys nigrinoda nigrinoda*
                     Graptemys nigrinoda delticola
Ringed map turtle *Graptemys oculifera*
Ouachita map turtle *Graptemys ouachitensis ouachitensis*
                     Graptemys ouachitensis sabinensis
False map turtle *Graptemys pseudogeographica pseudogeographica*
                     Graptemys pseudogeographica kohnii
Alabama map turtle *Graptemys pulchra*
Texas map turtle *Graptemys versa*
Diamondback terrapin *Malaclemys terrapin terrapin*
                     Malaclemys terrapin centrata
                     Malaclemys terrapin littoralis
                     Malaclemys terrapin macrospilota
                     Malaclemys terrapin pileata
                     Malaclemys terrapin rhizophorarum
                     Malaclemys terrapin tequesta
Alabama red-bellied turtle *Pseudemys alabamensis*
River cooter *Pseudemys concinna concinna*
                     Pseudemys concinna gorzugi
                     Pseudemys concinna hieroglyphica
                     Pseudemys concinna metteri
                     Pseudemys concinna suwanniensis
                     Pseudemys concinna texana
Coastal plain turtle *Pseudemys floridana floridana*
                     Pseudemys floridana peninsularis
Florida red-bellied turtle *Pseudemys nelsoni*
Red-bellied turtle *Pseudemys rubriventris*
Eastern box turtle *Terrapene carolina carolina*
                     Terrapene carolina bauri
                     Terrapene carolina major

Terrapene carolina mexicana
Terrapene carolina triunguis
Terrapene carolina yucatana
Coahuilan box turtle *Terrapene coahuila*
Nelson's box turtle *Terrapene nelsoni nelsoni*
Terrapene nelsoni klauberi
Ornate box turtle *Terrapene ornata ornata*
Terrapene ornata luteola
Hispanolan slider *Trachemys decorata*
North Antillean slider *Trachemys decussata decussata*
Trachemys decussata angusta
Trachemys decussata granti
Trachemys decussata plana
Black-bellied slider *Trachemys dorbignyi*
Common slider *Trachemys scripta scripta*
Trachemys scripta brasiliensis
Trachemys scripta callirostris
Trachemys scripta cataspila
Trachemys scripta chichiriviche
Trachemys scripta elegans
Trachemys scripta gaigeae
Trachemys scripta grayi
Trachemys scripta hiltoni
Trachemys scripta nebulosa
Trachemys scripta ornata
Trachemys scripta taylori
Trachemys scripta troostii
Trachemys scripta venusta
Trachemys scripta yaquia
Puerto Rican slider *Trachemys stejnegeri stejnegeri*
Trachemys stejnegeri malonei
Trachemys stejnegeri vicina
Jamaican slider *Trachemys terrapen terrapen*
Trachemys terrapen felis

Subfamily Batagurinae

Annam leaf turtle *Annamemys annamensis*
Batagur *Batagur baska*
Biuku *Callagur borneoensis*
Chinese red-necked pond turtle *Chinemys kwangtungensis*
Chinese broad-headed pond turtle *Chinemys megalocephala*
Reeves' turtle *Chinemys reevesi*
Amboina box turtle *Cuora amboinensis*
Snake-eating turtle *Cuora flavomarginata*
Indochinese box turtle *Cuora galbinifrons*
Three-banded box turtle *Cuora trifasciata*
Yunnan box turtle *Cuora yunnanensis*
Leaf turtle *Cyclemys dentata*

Jagged-shell turtle *Cyclemys mouhoti*
Black pond turtle *Geoclemys hamiltonii*
Black-breasted leaf turtle *Geoemyda spengleri spengleri*
          Geoemyda spengleri japonica
Brahminy river turtle *Hardella thurji*
Arakan forest turtle *Heosemys depressa*
Giant Asian pond turtle *Heosemys grandis*
Leyte pond turtle *Heosemys leytensis*
Cochin forest cane turtle *Heosemys silvatica*
Spiny turtle *Heosemys spinosa*
Yellow-headed temple turtle *Hieremys annandalii*
Three-striped roofed turtle *Kachuga dhongoka*
Red-crowned roofed turtle *Kachuga kachuga*
Brown-roofed turtle *Kachuga smithii*
Assam roofed turtle *Kachuga sylhetensis*
Indian roofed turtle *Kachuga tecta*
Indian tent turtle *Kachuga tentoria tentoria*
        Kachuga tentoria circumdata
Burmese roofed turtle *Kachuga trivittata*
Snail-eating turtle *Malayemys subtrijuga*
Caspian turtle *Mauremys caspica caspica*
      Mauremys caspica leprosa
      Mauremys caspica rivulata
Japanese turtle *Mauremys japonica*
Asian yellow pond turtle *Mauremys nigricans*
Tricarinate hill turtle *Melanochelys tricarinata*
Indian black turtle *Melanochelys trijuga trijuga*
       Melanochelys trijuga coronata
       Melanochelys trijuga edeniana
       Melanochelys trijuga indopeninsularis
       Melanochelys trijuga parkeri
       Melanochelys trijuga thermalis
Burmese eyed turtle *Morenia ocellata*
Indian eyed turtle *Morenia petersi*
Malayan flat-shelled turtle *Notochelys platynota*
Chinese striped-necked turtle *Ocadia sinesis*
Malaysian giant turtle *Orlitia borneensis*
Brown wood turtle *Rhinoclemmys annulata*
Furrowed wood turtle *Rhinoclemmys areolata*
Maracaibo wood turtle *Rhinoclemmys diademata*
Black wood turtle *Rhinoclemmys funerea*
Colombian wood turtle *Rhinoclemmys melanosterna*
Large-nosed wood turtle *Rhinoclemmys nasuta*
Painted wood turtle *Rhinoclemmys pulcherrima pulcherrima*
      Rhinoclemmys pulcherrima incisa
      Rhinoclemmys pulcherrima manni
      Rhinoclemmys pulcherrima rogerbarbouri
Spotted-legged turtle *Rhinoclemmys punctularia*

Mexican spotted wood turtle *Rhinoclemmys rubida rubida*
                                    Rhinoclemmys rubida perixantha
Eyed turtle *Sacalia bealei*
Siamese temple turtle *Siebenrockiella crassicollis*

American mud and musk turtles: family Kinosternidae

Narrow-bridged musk turtle *Claudius angustatus*
Tabasco mud turtle *Kinosternon acutum*
Alamos mud turtle *Kinosternon alamose*
Central American mud turtle *Kinosternon angustipons*
Striped mud turtle *Kinosternon bauri*
Creaser's mud turtle *Kinosternon creaseri*
Colombian mud turtle *Kinosternon dunni*
Yellow mud turtle *Kinosternon flavescens flavescens*
                               Kinosternon flavescens arizonense
                               Kinosternon flavescens durangoense
                               Kinosternon flavescens spooneri
Herrara's mud turtle *Kinosternon herrerai*
Mexican rough-footed mud turtle *Kinosternon hirtipes hirtipes*
                               Kinosternon hirtipes chapalaense
                               Kinosternon hirtipes magdalense
                               Kinsternon hirtipes megacephalum
                               Kinosternon hirtipes murrayi
                               Kinosternon hirtipes tarascense
Mexican mud turtle *Kinosternon integrum*
White-lipped mud turtle *Kinosternon leucostomum leucostomum*
                               Kinosternon leucostomum postinguinale
Oaxaca mud turtle *Kinosternon oaxacae*
Scorpion mud turtle *Kinosternon scorpioides scorpioides*
                               Kinosternon scorpioides abaxillare
                               Kinosternon scorpioides albogulare
                               Kinosternon scorpioides carajasensis
                               Kinosternon scorpioides cruentatum
                               Kinosternon scorpioides seriei
Sonoran mud turtle *Kinosternon sonoriense*
Common mud turtle *Kinosternon subrubrum subrubrum*
                               Kinosternon subrubrum hippocrepis
                               Kinosternon subrubrum steindachneri
Chiapas giant musk turtle *Staurotypus salvinii*
Mexican giant musk turtle *Staurotypus triporcatus*
Razor-backed musk turtle *Sternotherus carinatus*
Loggerhead musk turtle *Sternotherus minor minor*
                               Sternotherus minor depressus
                               Sternotherus minor peltifer
Stinkpot turtle *Sternotherus odoratus*

Big-headed turtle: family Platysternidae

Big-headed turtle *Platysternon megacephalum megacephalum*
     Platysternon megacephalum peguense
     Platysternon megacephalum tristornalis
     Platysternon megacephalum vogeli

Tortoises: family Testudinidae

South African bowsprit tortoise *Chersina angulata*
Star tortoise *Geochelone (Geochelone) elegans*
Leopard tortoise *Geochelone (Geochelone) pardalis pardalis*
     Geochelone (Geochelone) pardalis babcocki
Burmese star tortoise *Geochelone (Geochelone) platynota*
African spurred tortoise *Geochelone (Geochelone) sulcata*
Aldabran giant tortoise *Geochelone (Aldabrachelys) gigantea*
Radiated tortoise *Geochelone (Asterochelys) radiata*
Madagascan tortoise *Geochelone (Asterochelys) yniphora*
Red-fooded tortoise *Geochelone (Chelonoidis) carbonaria*
Chilean tortoise *Geochelone (Chelonoidis) chilensis*
Yellow-footed tortoise *Geochelone (Chelonoidis) denticulata*
Cerro Azul giant tortoise *Geochelone (Chelonoidis) elephantopus elephantopus*
Abingdon Island giant tortoise *Geochelone (Chelonoidis) elephantopus abingdoni*
Cape Berkeley giant tortoise *Geochelone (Chelonoidis) elephantopus becki*
Chatham Island giant tortoise *Geochelone (Chelonoidis) elephantopus chathamensis*
James Island giant tortoise *Geochelone (Chelonoidis) elephantopus darwini*
Duncan Island giant tortoise *Geochelone (Chelonoidis) elephantopus ephippium*
Sierra Negra giant tortoise *Geochelone (Chelonoidis) elephantopus guntheri*
Hood Island giant tortoise *Geochelone (Chelonoidis) elephantopus hoodensis*
Volcan Darwin giant tortoise *Geochelone (Chelonoidis) elephantopus microphyes*
Fernandina Island giant tortoise *Geochelone (Chelonoidis) elephantopus phantastica*
Indefatigable Island giant tortoise *Geochelone (Chelonoidis) elephantopus porteri*
Volcan Alcedo giant tortoise *Geochelone (Chelonoidis) elephantopus vandenburghi*
Elongated tortoise *Geochelone (Indotestudo) elongata*
Travancore tortoise *Geochelone (Indotestudo) travancorica*
Brown tortoise *Geochelone (Manouria) emys emys*
     Geochelone (Manouria) emys phayeri
Impressed tortoise *Geochelone (Manouria) impressa*
Californian Desert tortoise *Gopherus agassizii*
Texas gopher tortoise *Gopherus berlandieri*
Mexican gopher tortoise *Gopherus flavomarginatus*
Florida gopher tortoise *Gopherus polyphemus*
Parrot-beaked tortoise *Homopus areolatus*
Donner-weer tortoise *Homopus boulengeri*

Karroo tortoise *Homopus femoralis*
Speckled Cape tortoise *Homopus signatus*
Bell's hingeback tortoise *Kinixys belliana belliana*
                                Kinixys belliana nogueyi
Eroded hingeback tortoise *Kinixys erosa*
Home's hingeback tortoise *Kinixys homeana*
Pancake tortoise *Malacochersus tornieri*
Geometric tortoise *Psammobates geometricus*
Serrated tortoise *Psammobates oculifera*
Tent tortoise *Psammobates tentorius tentorius*
                        Psammobates tentorius trimeni
                        Psammobates tentorius verroxii
Madagascan spider tortoise *Pyxis arachnoides*
Madagascan flat-tailed tortoise *Pyxis planicauda*
Mediterranean spur-thighed tortoise *Testudo (Testudo) graeca graeca*
                                Testudo (Testudo) graeca terrestris
                                Testudo (Testudo) graeca zarudnyi
Hermann's tortoise *Testudo (Testudo) hermanni hermanni*
                        Testudo (Testudo) hermanni robertmertensi
Horsfield's tortoise *Testudo (Testudo) horsfieldii*
Marginated tortoise *Testudo (Testudo) marginata*
Egyptian tortoise *Testudo (Pseudotestudo) kleinmanni*

Soft-shelled turtles: family Trionychidae

Subfamily Cyclanorbinae

Nubian soft-shelled turtle *Cyclanorbis elegans*
Senegal soft-shelled turtle *Cyclanorbis senegalensis*
Aubry's soft-shelled turtle *Cycloderma aubryi*
Zambezi soft-shelled turtle *Cycloderma frenatum*
Indian flap-shelled turtle *Lissemys punctata punctata*
                                Lissemys punctata andersoni
Burmese flap-shelled turtle *Lissemys scutata*

Subfamily Trionychinae

Narrow-headed soft-shelled turtle *Chitra indica*
Asian giant soft-shelled turtle *Pelochelys bibroni*
Black-rayed soft-shelled turtle *Trionyx cartilagineus*
Euphrates soft-shelled turtle *Trionyx euphraticus*
Florida soft-shelled turtle *Trionyx ferox*
Burmese soft-shelled turtle *Trionyx formosus*
Ganges soft-shelled turtle *Trionyx gangeticus*
Peacock soft-shelled turtle *Trionyx hurum*
Nagpur soft-shelled turtle *Trionyx leithii*
Smooth soft-shelled turtle *Trionyx muticus muticus*
                                Trionyx muticus calvatus

Black soft-shelled turtle *Trionyx nigricans*
Chinese soft-shelled turtle *Trionyx sinensis sinensis*
Eastern spiny soft-shelled turtle *Trionyx spiniferus spiniferus*
Gulf Coast soft-shelled turtle *Trionyx spiniferus asper*
Texas spiny soft-shelled turtle *Trionyx spiniferus emoryi*
Guadalupe spiny soft-shelled turtle *Trionyx spiniferus guadalupensis*
Western spiny soft-shelled turtle *Trionyx spiniferus hartwegi*
Pallid spiny soft-shelled turtle *Trionyx spiniferus pallidus*
Wattle-necked soft-shelled turtle *Trionyx steindachneri*
Swinhoe's soft-shelled turtle *Trionyx swinhoei*
Malayan soft-shelled turtle *Trionyx subplanus*
Nile soft-shelled turtle *Trionyx triunguis*

Side-necked turtles: sub-order Pleurodira

Snake-necked turtles: family Chelidae

Giant snake-necked turtle *Chelodina expansa*
Common snake-necked turtle *Chelodina longicollis*
New Guinea snake-necked turtle *Chelodina novaeguineae*
Narrow-breasted snake-necked turtle *Chelodina oblonga*
Parker's snake-necked turtle *Chelodina parkeri*
North Australian snake-necked turtle *Chelodina rugosa*
Siebenrock's snake-necked turtle *Chelodina siebenrocki*
Dinner-plate turtle *Chelodina steindachneri*
Mata mata *Chelus fimbriatus*
Northern Australian snapping turtle *Elseya dentata*
Saw-shelled snapping turtle *Elseya latisternum*
New Guinea snapping turtle *Elseya novaeguineae*
Australian big-headed side-necked turtle *Emydura australis*
Krefft's river turtle *Emydura kreffti*
Murray River turtle *Emydura macquarrii*
Brisbane short-necked turtle *Emydura signata*
Red-bellied short-necked turtle *Emydura subglobosa*
Victoria short-necked turtle *Emydura victoriae*
Maximilian's snake-headed turtle *Hydromedusa maximiliani*
South American snake-headed turtle *Hydromedusa tectifera*
Geoffrey's side-necked turtle *Phrynops (Phrynops) geoffroanus geoffroanus*
                               Phrynops (Phrynops) geoffroanus tuberosus
Hilaire's side-necked turtle *Phrynops (Phrynops) hilarii*
Hoge's side-necked turtle *Phrynops (Phrynops) hogei*
Red-footed Amazon side-necked turtle *Phrynops (Phrynops) rufipes*
Williams' South American side-necked turtle *Phrynops (Phrynops) williamsi*
Dahl's toad-headed turtle *Phrynops (Batrachemys) dahli*
Common toad-headed turtle *Phrynops (Batrachemys) nasutus nasutus*
Western toad-headed turtle *Phrynops (Batrachemys) nasutus wermuthi*
Tuberculate toad-headed turtle *Phrynops (Batrachemys) tuberculatus*
Zulia toad-headed turtle *Phrynops (Batrachemys) zuliae*

Vanderhaege's toad-headed turtle *Phrynops (Batrachemys) vanderhaegei*
Gibba turtle *Phrynops (Mesoclemmys) gibbus*
Big-headed Pantanal swamp turtle *Platemys macrocephala*
Chaco side-necked turtle *Platemys pallidipectoris*
Twist-neck turtle *Platemys platycephala*
Brazilian radiolated swamp turtle *Platemys radiolata*
Black spine-necked swamp turtle *Platemys spixii*
Western swamp turtle *Pseudemydura umbrina*
Fitzroy turtle *Rheodytes leukops*

Afro-American sidenecks: family Pelomedusidae

Madagascan big-headed side-necked turtle *Erymnochelys madagascariensis*
Helmeted turtle *Pelomedusa subrufa subrufa*
                    Pelomedusa subrufa olivacea
Big-headed Amazon River turtle *Peltocephalus dumerilianus*
Adanson's turtle *Pelusios adansonii*
Okavango mud turtle *Pelusios bechuanicus*
African keeled mud turtle *Pelusios carinatus*
African mud turtle *Pelusios castaneus castaneus*
                    Pelusios castaneus castanoides
                    Pelusios castaneus chapini
                    Pelusios castaneus derbianus
                    Pelusios castaneus rhodesianus
Gabon turtle *Pelusios gabonensis*
African dwarf mud turtle *Pelusios nanus*
West African black forest turtle *Pelusios niger*
Serrated turtle *Pelusios sinuatus*
East African black mud turtle *Pelusios subniger*
Upemba mud turtle *Pelusios upembae*
Williams' African mud turtle *Pelusios williamsi williamsi*
                    Pelusios williamsi laurenti
                    Pelusios williamsi lutescens
Red-headed Amazon side-necked turtle *Podocnemis erythrocephala*
Arrau River turtle *Podocnemis expansa*
Rio Magdalena River turtle *Podocnemis lewyana*
Six-tubercled Amazon River turtle *Podocnemis sextuberculata*
Yellow-spotted Amazon River turtle *Podocnemis unifilis*
Savanna side-necked turtle *Podocnemis vogli*

Glossary

Abdominal scutes Scutes located third from the front on the plastron. Usually the largest.

Aestivate Means of surviving unfavourable environmental conditions by inactivity.

Amphicoelous A vertebra with a socket at either end.

Anaerobic Surviving without oxygen.

Anal scutes Those at the rear of the plastron.

Annuli Pattern of so-called annual growth rings on the carapace, associated with tortoises.

Axillary scutes Those where the front limbs protrude from the shell, on the plastron.

Bridges The vertical sides of the shell, where the carapace joins the plastron.

Carapace The upper part of the shell above the bridges.

Caruncle The sharp projection on the nose of hatching chelonians, enabling them to break out of the shell. Also known as the 'egg tooth'.

Central scutes Those running down the midline of the carapace.

Cloaca The chamber close to the anal opening where urinary, digestive and reproductive tracts converge.

Costal scutes Those running on both sides of the centrals, on the carapace.

Digitigrade Only the digits carry the weight when the animal is moving.

Femoral scutes Located next to the anal scutes on the plastron, close to the hind legs.

Girdles Provide support for fore and hind limbs.

Gular scute(s) At the front of the plastron. May be single in certain cases.

Humeral scutes Located just behind the gular scute(s) at the front of the plastron.

Inframarginal scutes Link the marginal scutes with those of the plastron.

Inguinal scutes In front of the hind limbs.

Intergular scute This divides the gular scutes.

Kyphosis Abnormal growth, notably the swelling of the carapace typically associated with soft-shelled turtles.

Lamina(e) Redundant description for scute(s).

Lateral scutes Costal scutes.

Marginal scutes Those located around the edge of the carapace.

Melanism Darkening of coloration, caused by the presence of melanin pigment.

Nuchal scute Located at the front of the carapace in the midline, if present.

Occipital region At the back of the skull.

Papilla(e) Raised areas of soft tissue.

Pectoral scutes Connect to the humeral scutes on the plastron.

Plastron Lower part of the shell, beneath the bridges.

Quadrate Bone which provides the articulating surface for the bottom jaw, located at the back of the skull.

Supracaudal scutes Pair of rear marginal scutes, which are fused in some cases.

Suture The resulting jagged patterning where shell bones fuse together.

Unguligrade A gait in which only the claws touch the ground when walking.

Vertebral scutes Central scutes.

Xiphiplastra Back pair of bones in the plastron.

Guide to Further Reading

Few books are devoted to chelonians, and the following list contains a number which are out of print. You may be able to obtain these from your local library, however, or from a specialist natural history book dealer.

Alderton, D. (1986) *A Petkeeper's Guide to Reptiles & Amphibians*, Salamander Books, London.

Behler, J. L. & King, F. W. (1979) *The Audubon Society Field Guide to North American Reptiles & Amphibians*, Alfred A. Knopf, New York.

Bellairs, A. d'A. (1969) *The Life of Reptiles*, Weidenfeld & Nicolson, London.

Bellairs, A. d'A. & Cox, C. B. (Eds) (1976) *Morphology & Biology of Reptiles*, Academic Press, London.

Carr, A. (1952) *Handbook of Turtles*, Cornell University Press, Ithaca, New York.

Carr, A. (1968) *The Turtle: A Natural History*, Cassell & Co., London.

Cogger, H. G. (1983) *Reptiles & Amphibians of Australia*, A. H. & A. W. Reed, Sydney.

Conant, R. (1975) *A Field Gude to Reptiles & Amphibians of Eastern & Central America*, Houghton Mifflin & Co., Boston.

Cook, F. R. (1984) *Introduction to Canadian Amphibians and Reptiles*, National Museums of Canada, Ottawa.

Cooper, J. E. & Jackson, O. F. (1981) *Diseases of Reptilia, Vols. 1–2*, Academic Press, London.

Daniel, J. C. (1983) *The Book of Indian Reptiles*, Bombay Natural History Society, Bombay.

Ernst, C. H. & Babour, R. W. (1973) *Turtles of the United States*, University Press of Lexington, Kentucky.

Gans, C. et al. (1969–82) *Biology of the Reptilia, Vols 1–13*, Academic Press, London.

Goode, J. (1967) *Freshwater Tortoises of Australia & New Guinea (in the Family Chelidae)*, Lansdowne Press, Melbourne.

Groombridge, B. (1982) *The IUCN Amphibia-Reptilia Red Data Book part 1*, IUCN, Gland, Switzerland.

Harless, M. & Morlock, H. (Eds) (1979) *Turtles: Perspectives & Research*, John Wiley & Sons, New York.

Iverson, J. B. (1986) *A Checklist with Distribution Maps of the Turtles of the World* (Privately printed), Richmond, Indiana.

Mao, S.-H. (1971) *Turtles of Taiwan*, Commercial Press, Taipei.

Murphy, J. B. & Collins, J. T. (Eds.) (1980) *Reproductive Biology & Diseases of Captive Reptiles*, Society for the Study of Reptiles & Amphibians (SSAR), Ohio.

Pritchard, P. C. H. (1979) *Encyclopedia of Turtles*, T. F. H. Publications, New Jersey.

Pritchard, P. C. H. & Trebbau, P. (1984) *The Turtles of Venezuela* SSAR, Ohio.

Schmidt, K. P. & Inger, R. F. (1957) *Living Reptiles of the World*, Doubleday & Co., New York.

Smith, H. M. & Brodie, E. D. Jr. (1982) *A Guide to Field Identification. Reptiles of North America.* Golden Press, New York.

Stebbins, R. C. (1985) *A Field Guide to Western Reptiles & Amphibians*, Houghton Mifflin & Co., Boston.

Welch, K. R. G. (1982) *Herpetology of Africa: A Checklist and Bibliography*, Krieger Publishing, Florida.

Welch, K. R. G. (1983) *Herpetology of Europe & South-west Asia: A Checklist and Bibliography*, Krieger Publishing, Florida.

Wirot, N. (1979) *The Turtles of Thailand*, Siamfarm Zoological Garden, Bangkok.

Zappalorti, R. T. (1976) *The Amateur Zoologist's Guide to Turtles & Crocodilians*, Stackpole Books, Pennsylvania.

Herpetological journals also regularly feature information about chelonians. Details of these publications worldwide can be found in *Herpetological Circular no. 13* (1983), SSAR, Ohio.

Index

Figures in **bold** refer to page numbers of illustrations